T0212852

Adoption and Assisted Reproduction in Germany

Family Law in a Global Society

Editor-in-Chief

Sanford N. Katz (*Boston College*)

Associate Editors

Volumes published in this Brill Research Perspective are listed at *brill.com/rpfl*

Adoption and Assisted Reproduction in Germany

Legal Framework and Current Issues

By

Saskia Lettmaier

BRILL

LEIDEN | BOSTON

This paperback book edition is simultaneously published as Volume 1.4 (2016), in *Family Law in a Global Society*, DOI:10.1163/24058386-12340004.

Library of Congress Control Number: 2019931568

Typeface for the Latin, Greek, and Cyrillic scripts: "Brill". See and download: brill.com/brill-typeface.

ISBN 978-90-04-33981-1 (paperback)
ISBN 978-90-04-33992-7 (e-book)

Contents

Adoption and Assisted Reproduction in Germany: Legal Framework and Current Issues

Saskia Lettmaier
Christian-Albrechts-Universität zu Kiel, Kiel, Germany
slettmaier@law.uni-kiel.de

Abstract

In Germany, as elsewhere, couples and individuals suffering from unwanted childlessness have two principal means to overcome it. One, adoption, has existed and been quite heavily regulated for centuries. The other, assisted reproduction, has only recently come into its own and has not yet been comprehensively dealt with by the German legislature.

This monograph provides a survey of adoption and assisted reproduction as alternative (non-coital) ways of establishing parent-child relationships in Germany. Part 1 on adoption sets out the current regulatory framework and discusses a number of recent 'hot topics,' including adult and stepparent adoptions.

Unlike for adoption, there is little state regulation for assisted reproduction in Germany. Most of the complex legal issues are dealt with by professional self-regulation and ordinary family-law rules. Part 2 sets out what forms of assisted reproduction are currently permitted; who has access to them; and how parental status is allocated. It also discusses the child's right to know its genetic origins; the risks to donors; and the implications of 'reproductive tourism.'

Keywords

adoption – stepparent adoption – adult adoption – same-sex partner adoption – co-parent adoption – parental status – reproductive technologies – right to know one's genetic origins – reproductive tourism – surrogacy – sperm donation – artificial insemination

List of Abbreviations

AcP	*Archiv für civilistische Praxis*
AdVermiG	*Adoptionsvermittlungsgesetz*
AG	Amtsgericht
ALR	*Allgemeines Landrecht für die Preussischen Staaten*
BayObLG	Bayerisches Oberstes Landesgericht
BeckOK	Beck'scher Online-Kommentar
BGB	*Bürgerliches Gesetzbuch*
BGBl.	*Bundesgesetzblatt*
BGH	Bundesgerichtshof
BR-Drucks.	Bundesrat-Drucksache
BT-Drucks.	Bundestag-Drucksache
BVerfG	Bundesverfassungsgericht
DNotZ	*Deutsche Notar-Zeitschrift*
ECHR	European Convention on Human Rights
ECtHR	European Court of Human Rights
EGBGB	*Einführungsgesetz zum Bürgerlichen Gesetzbuch*
ErbStG	Erbschaftssteuergesetz
ESchG	*Embryonenschutzgesetz*
EU	European Union
FamFG	Gesetz über das Verfahren in Familiensachen und in Angelegenheiten der freiwilligen Gerichtsbarkeit
FamRZ	*Zeitschrift für das gesamte Familienrecht*
FuR	*Familie und Recht*
GG	Grundgesetz
GVG	Gerichtsverfassungsgesetz
JuS	*Juristische Schulung*
KG	Kammergericht
LG	Landgericht
LPartG	Lebenspartnerschaftsgesetz
MünchKomm	Münchener Kommentar
NJW	*Neue Juristische Wochenschrift*
No.	Number
NZFam	*Neue Zeitschrift für Familienrecht*
OLG	Oberlandesgericht
RegE	Regierungsentwurf
RNotZ	*Rheinische Notar-Zeitschrift*
SaRegG	*Samenspenderregistergesetz*

Sent.	Sentence
StAZ	*Das Standesamt*
ZNR	*Zeitschrift für neuere Rechtsgeschichte*
ZRP	*Zeitschrift für Rechtspolitik*

Introduction

In Germany, as elsewhere, couples and individuals suffering from unwanted childlessness have two principal means of overcoming it. One—adoption—has existed and been quite heavily regulated in Germany for centuries. The other—assisted reproduction—has only recently come into its own with advances in medical technology, and has not yet been comprehensively dealt with by the German legislature. This monograph provides a two-part survey of adoption and assisted reproduction as alternative (non-coital) ways of establishing parent–child relationships in Germany.

Part 1, on *adoption*, briefly discusses the history of the institution before setting out the current legal framework: from the conditions that have to be met for an adoption decree to be made, to the legal effects of adoption, and the circumstances under which an adoption decree can be set aside. It also discusses a number of controversial 'hot topics,' including, but not limited to, adult, same-sex partner, and stepparent adoptions.

Unlike the position on adoption, there is still relatively little state regulation of assisted reproduction in Germany. So far, the German legislature has largely confined itself to criminalizing certain reproductive methodologies (such as egg donation and surrogacy). As a result, most of the complex legal issues arising from assisted reproductive technologies—in particular, questions of access and the allocation of parental status—are dealt with by professional self-regulation and ordinary family law rules. *Part 2* of this monograph sets out what forms of *assisted reproduction* are currently permitted in Germany; who has access to them; and who is or may be recognized (and by what means) as the legal parent(s) of a child born of assisted reproductive technologies. This part also discusses the constitutionally protected right to know one's genetic origins, as it relates to children of assisted reproduction; the position of and risks to sperm donors; and the national implications of 'reproductive tourism'—in particular, the recognition of foreign surrogacy arrangements by German courts. It concludes by looking at some recent proposals for reforming this area of the law.

Part 1: Adoption

1   *A Brief History of Adoption with Particular Reference to Germany*
Adoption is a legal institution with a long history. Today, in most countries, it
is a mechanism designed for the care of (usually young) children, whose biological parents are unavailable, unable, unwilling, or unfit to provide for them.
In the words of the parliamentary document accompanying the draft German
Adoption Act of 1976 (which continues to be the chief source of the current
law of adoption in Germany), the purpose of adoption is to provide families
for children who lack a healthy home.[1] If one investigates the historical roots of
the institution, which extend back to pre-Christian times, however, one finds
that early adoption laws did not have this child-centered orientation: adoptions in ancient Greece or Rome, for instance, typically served the (religious,
political, economic, etc.) motives of the adopter rather than the welfare of the
adoptee.[2]

The German law of adoption was shaped by three chief influences: that of
Roman law, that of Germanic law, and that of the church.

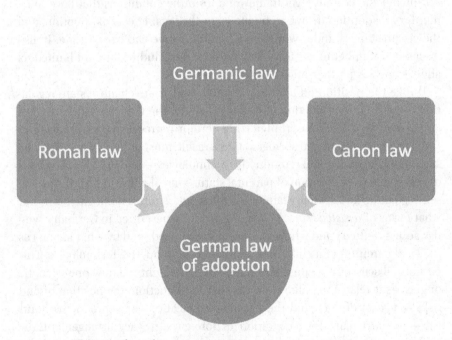

FIGURE 1   Illustration by author

---

1   BT-Drucks. 7/3061, 1.
2   Christiane Kunst, *Römische Adoption: Zur Strategie einer Familienorganisation* (Frankfurt:
    Marthe Clauss, 2006), 49, 273, 293.

The last two influences shared a conception of the family that privileged blood relationships and natural procreation within legitimate marriage over the artificial ties created by adoption.[3] When the three influences were blended together in the medieval *ius commune*, the result was a restrictive law of adoption, which was little used.[4]

Medieval German law books such as the *Sachsenspiegel* of 1235,[5] for instance, did not contain any rules on adoption. And while adoption was included in the big eighteenth-century codes (such as the Bavarian *Codex Maximilianeus Bavaricus Civilis* and the Prussian *Allgemeines Landrecht* (or 'ALR')), this was not on account of the institution's practical importance, but on account of the codifiers' aim of achieving a 'gapless' exposition of the law.[6] Moreover, the rules on adoption that the codes contained were quite restrictive.[7]

This restrictive regime served as a model for the adoption law of the German Civil Code, the *Bürgerliches Gesetzbuch* (or 'BGB') of 1900. The original BGB required a minimum age of fifty years (subject to dispensation) and childlessness on the part of the adoptive parent and limited the legal effects of the adoption order to the adoptive parent and child inter se. The adoption did not terminate the adoptee's legal ties with its birth family, nor did it establish new ties between the adoptee and the adoptive parent's spouse and wider family.

In practical terms, the institution continued to lead a marginal existence (with only about one thousand adoptions per year[8]) for several decades after the BGB 1900 entered into force. It was not until the two world wars and their disastrous consequences that the number of adoptions increased and that the law of adoption itself acquired its modern child-centered orientation.[9]

---

3 Michael Sheehan, "The European Family and Canon Law," *Continuity and Change* 6, 3 (1991): 355.

4 Medieval and early modern treatises on adoption called for a high minimum age and childlessness on the part of adoptive parents. See, e.g., Tancred, *Summa de matrimonio*, ed. Agathon Wunderlich (Göttingen, 1841), 39; Joachim Mynsinger von Frundeck, *Apoteslesma, sive corpus perfectum Scholiorum ad quatuor libros Institutionum Iuris civilis* (Basel, 1555), 46; Hugo Donellus, *Opera Omnia: cum Notis Oswaldi Hilligeri* (Florence, 1840–47), vol. 1, lib. 2, cap. 23, p. 6.

5 Clausdieter Schott, "Sachsenspiegel und Adoption—die Macht der Glosse," ZNR (2011): 4.

6 Clausdieter Schott, *Kindesannahme—Adoption—Wahlkindschaft: Rechtsgeschichte und Rechtsgeschichten* (Frankfurt: Wolfgang Metzner, 2009), 196.

7 See, e.g., §§ 668–69, 671, 701, 708–12 ALR.

8 Manfred Schnitzerling, "Die Fortentwicklung der Adoption seit der Jahrhundertwende," StAZ (1960): 57.

9 Schnitzerling, "Die Fortentwicklung der Adoption seit der Jahrhundertwende," 57.

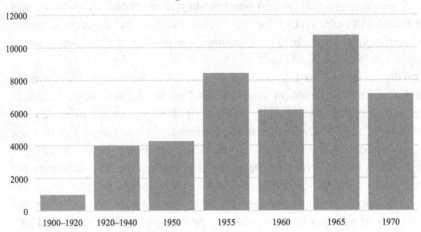

FIGURE 2
SOURCE: SCHNITZERLING, "DIE FORTENTWICKLUNG DER ADOPTION SEIT DER
JAHRHUNDERTWENDE," 57 *ET SEQQ*

To take care of the many children orphaned by war, the high eligibility thresh-
olds were successively reduced. In 1950, childlessness (like the minimum age
of fifty years before it) became a dispensable requirement.[10] In 1961, the adoption of minors was made the central case of adoption. The court could, by way
of exception, allow the adoption of an adult, but only if the adult adoption
seemed morally justified.[11] At the same time, the minimum age was lowered
to thirty-five years and continued to be dispensable.[12] In 1973, it was further
reduced to (the current minimum of) twenty-five years[13] to make sure that
the adoptive parents were of a suitable age for the (now predominantly very
young) adoptees.[14] The adoption of stepchildren and of the adopter's own
illegitimate children was privileged.[15] To tackle the dangers of long-term in-
stitutional and foster care, it became possible to order an adoption against
the wishes of the biological parents.[16] At the same time, the legal effects of

10   *Gesetz zur Erleichterung der Annahme an Kindes Statt* of May 8, 1950, BGBl. I, 356.
11   §§ 1744 sent. 3, 1745c BGB 1961.
12   *Familienrechtsänderungsgesetz* of August 11, 1961, BGBl. I, 1221.
13   *Gesetz zur Änderung der Vorschriften des Adoptionsrechtes, Vorabnovelle* of August 14, 1973,
      BGBl. I, 1013.
14   BT-Drucks. 7/421, 4.
15   *Familienrechtsänderungsgesetz* of August 11, 1961, BGBl. I, 1221; *Gesetz über die recht-
      liche Stellung der nichtehelichen Kinder* of August 19, 1969, BGBl. I, 1243; *Gesetz über die
      Annahme als Kind und zur Änderung anderer Vorschriften, Adoptionsgesetz* of July 2,
      1976, BGBl. I, 1749.
16   *Familienrechtsänderungsgesetz* of August 11, 1961, BGBl. I, 1221.

adoption were expanded. Even before the Second World War, the courts had de facto loosened the ties between the adoptee and its birth family by sanctioning incognito adoptions.[17] The natural termination point of this development came in 1976, with the legal transition to full adoption.[18] The drafters of the Adoption Act of July 2, 1976 believed that adoptees had to feel as though they were an integral part of their adoptive families for their optimal development. This required that their legal status be identical to that of a natural child.[19] Hence, their legal ties with their birth families were completely severed (§ 1755 BGB) and the law treated them as the natural offspring of the adoptive parent(s) and as related to their wider families (§ 1754 I, II BGB).

2 *The Current Legal Framework*
1 Requirements for an Adoption Decree

The current German law of adoption was shaped by the Adoption Act of July 2, 1976.[20] It is characterized by the following principles:

- an adoption has to be *decreed by a court* (*decree system*); it is not a matter for private negotiation and contracting between the interested parties;
- it generally[21] severs the adoptee's legal ties with the birth family and fully integrates the adoptee into the family of the adoptive parent(s) (*full adoption*);
- an adoption decree requires the *application and/or consent* of a number of interested parties;
- it can be granted only after a *home study* and only if a *substantive test* looking into the adoptee's best interests is satisfied.

a *Adoption Decree*

An adoption is *decreed* by a court on the *application* of the prospective parent(s) (§ 1752 BGB) and with the consent of a number of specified parties (see *infra* 1.b). The initiative lies with the adoptive parent(s). The application has to be notarized. It can be made only in person and must not contain any conditions or stipulations as to time (§ 1752 II BGB). Generally, the applicant has to be over twenty-five years old. However, an age limit of twenty-one years applies to in-family adoptions or where the applicants are married and the other spouse is over twenty-five (§ 1743 sent. 1, 2 BGB).

---

17 Schnitzerling, "Die Fortentwicklung der Adoption seit der Jahrhundertwende," 59.
18 *Gesetz über die Annahme als Kind und zur Änderung anderer Vorschriften, Adoptionsgesetz* of July 2, 1976, BGBl. I, 1749.
19 BT-Drucks. 7/3061, 19.
20 BGBl. I, 1749.
21 The adoption of a minor always has this effect. An adult adoption generally does not, but the court may order otherwise: §§ 1770, 1772 BGB.

As a rule, spouses (which, since 2017, includes same-sex spouses) may apply for an adoption decree only jointly (§§ 1741 II 2, 1754 I BGB) unless one of them is the child's natural parent (see § 1741 II 4 BGB for further exceptions). One spouse may adopt the child of the other spouse, with the result that the child is legally considered the child of both (§§ 1741 II 3, 1754 I BGB—stepparent adoption). Since 2005, it has been possible to adopt the biological child of one's registered partner, so that the child becomes a child of both partners and lives under their joint parental care.[22] In 2014, it was expressly provided that a registered partner may also adopt the adopted child of his or her partner.[23] With that one exception, however, persons who are not married may only adopt alone (§ 1741 II 1 BGB). In particular, German law does not allow joint adoptions by unmarried couples[24] or registered partners (although it now allows joint adoptions by same-sex married couples). Except where a spouse or registered partner joins an adoption made by his or her partner before the marriage or registered partnership, a child may be adopted only once during the lifetime of the adoptive parent(s) (§ 1742 BGB).

b   *Required Consents*
The prior consent of the following people is required for an adoption decree:
- *the child* (§ 1746 BGB): where the child is under fourteen years, the legal representative acts for the child (§ 1746 I 2 BGB). Where the child is over fourteen and thus has limited legal capacity, the child has to act him- or herself, albeit with the legal representative's approval (§ 1746 I 3 BGB);
- *the child's natural parents* (§ 1747 BGB): the consent of the natural parents is needed irrespective of their marital status and of whether they have parental responsibility. They need not know the identity of the adoptive parents. Incognito adoptions are legal. To ensure that natural parents can make a free and unconstrained decision, the law provides that their consent may not validly be given until eight weeks after the child's birth (§ 1747 II 1 BGB). There is a limited exception for unmarried fathers, who may consent before the child's birth (§ 1747 III No. 1 BGB). Once given, the consent is irrevocable. It loses its force, however, if the adoption application is refused or withdrawn or if no adoption is decreed within the next three years (§ 1750 IV BGB). An *unmarried father*, whose legal parentage has not yet been established (by

---

22   *Lebenspartnerschaftsgesetz* (Registered Partnership Act) in connection with § 1754 I, III BGB.
23   BGBl. 2014 I, 786.
24   BGH, NJW, 2017, 1672. See also Herbert Grziwotz, "Recht auf Stiefkindadoption in faktischen Lebensgemeinschaften," NJW (2017): 1646.

an acknowledgment of paternity or a court order), is considered the father for the purposes of § 1747 BGB if he adduces prima facie evidence that he had intercourse with the child's mother during the period of conception (§ 1747 I 2 BGB). A *sperm donor* is also considered a father within the meaning of § 1747 I 2 BGB if he adduces prima facie evidence for his paternity.[25] To afford him an opportunity to do so, the family court has to notify him of the adoption proceedings. The court may dispense with such a notification only if it is clear that the donor has no interest in the proceedings because he has waived his paternal rights.[26] As a result, anonymous sperm donors generally do not have to be notified of adoption proceedings. In exceptional circumstances, a natural parent's consent may be *dispensed with* by the court: for instance, where a parent is permanently incapacitated or where his or her residence is permanently unknown (§ 1747 IV 1 BGB). According to the new § 1747 IV 2 BGB, the residence of a mother who has given birth confidentially is regarded as permanently unknown until she provides the necessary information for the child's birth record. The court can also replace a parent's consent where the child's welfare is in severe danger. This intrusion into the very center of parental rights requires a serious violation of parental duties, as § 1748 I BGB makes clear (for example, where a serious crime has been perpetrated against the child). Interestingly, § 1748 IV BGB sets a lower standard when it comes to replacing the consent of an unmarried father who does not have joint parental responsibility for the child. The court can replace his consent if the child would suffer a disproportionate disadvantage in the absence of an adoption. A disproportionate disadvantage generally requires that the adoption would be so beneficial for the child that a concerned parent would not insist on maintaining the legal tie.[27] If the unmarried father wants to prevent an adoption in this case, he has to apply for (sole or joint) parental responsibility pursuant to § 1671 II BGB or § 1626a II BGB. If he does so, an adoption can be decreed only after the court has first of all ruled on the father's application for parental responsibility (§ 1747 III No. 3 BGB);

– *the adoptive parent's spouse and (adult) adoptee's spouse* (§§ 1749, 1767 II 2 BGB): in the former case, the court may replace an unwilling spouse's consent unless the spouse's refusal is based on legitimate conflicting interests (§ 1749 I 2, 3 BGB).

---

25 BGH, NJW (2015): 1820.
26 BGH, NJW (2015): 1820.
27 BGH, NJW (2005): 1781.

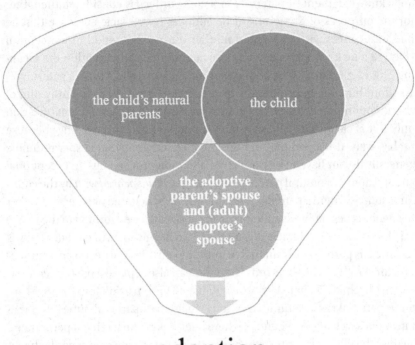

adoption

FIGURE 3   Illustration by author

The consent in question has to be given in person and has to be notarized. It must not contain any conditions or stipulations as to time (§ 1750 I-III BGB). A consent loses its effect if the adoption application is withdrawn or refused (§ 1750 IV BGB).

c   *Home Study*

Normally, an adoption will be ordered only if the child has previously lived with the prospective adoptive parent(s) for a reasonable amount of time (§ 1744 BGB). § 1751 BGB provides a legal framework for this home study. Once the natural parents consent to the adoption, their parental responsibility and rights to contact with the child are suspended. Generally,[28] the local youth welfare authority (Jugendamt) becomes the child's legal guardian. The prospective adoptive parents become entitled to decide routine matters and to represent the child legally to that extent (§§ 1751 I 4, 1688 I BGB). They also become liable for the child's maintenance (§ 1751 IV BGB).

---

28   The most significant exception relates to stepparent adoptions: see § 1751 II BGB.

d   *Substantive Requirements*

An adoption decree can be issued only if it benefits the child and if a true parent–child relationship between the parties is likely to develop (§ 1741 I 1 BGB). The decree cannot be issued if the adoption conflicts with the overriding interests of the adoptive parent's children or the adoptee's children, or if there is a danger to the adoptee's interests from the adoptive parent's children (§ 1745 sent. 1 BGB). Financial interests are not determinative (§ 1745 sent. 2 BGB).

2   The Adoption Decree and Its Legal Effects

Jurisdiction for adoption decrees lies with the *family court* (§ 23b I *Gerichtsverfassungsgesetz* (Judicature Act, 'GVG'; §§ 111 No. 4, 186-199 *Gesetz über das Verfahren in Familiensachen und in Angelegenheiten der freiwilligen* Gerichtsbarkeit (Family Court Act, 'FamFG')). Where the requirements for an adoption decree are met, the court will grant it after hearing the adoptive parent(s); the adoptee (§ 192 FamFG); their children, if any (§ 193 FamFG); and, where the adoptee is a minor, the local youth welfare office (§ 194 FamFG). Once made, an adoption decree is *final*. It can be neither revoked nor challenged (§ 197 III FamFG; see, however, *infra* 3.).

An adoption decree cannot be issued posthumously for a deceased child (§ 1753 I BGB). However, an adoption may be finalized after the death of the prospective adoptive parent if the parent filed the application or requested a notary to file the notarized application before his or her death. A posthumous adoption has retroactive effect and dates back to the time of the applicant's death (§ 1753 III BGB). It has the same legal effects as an adoption finalized during the adoptive parent's lifetime (§ 1753 III BGB).

Once an adoption order comes into effect, the adopted child is *legally considered the child of the adoptive parent(s)* and a member of the adoptive family (§ 1754 I, II BGB). This status confers statutory rights to inheritance, maintenance, etc. in the new family. At the same time, the child's *legal ties to the natural parents and their families are normally severed* (§ 1755 I BGB). This is not true, however, for *stepparent adoptions* by spouses or registered partners. In this case, only the child's ties to the outside parent and his or her relatives are cut (§ 1755 II BGB).[29] Where the adoptive parents are related to the child (by blood or marriage) in the second or third degree (as in an adoption by an uncle), only the legal ties to the birth parents, but not those to other members of the child's birth family, are terminated (§ 1756 BGB).

---

29   Where the outside parent has died and had parental responsibility, the ties with that parent's relatives are not cut: § 1756 II BGB.

The *child's last name* changes upon adoption and becomes the adoptive parent's family name (§ 1757 I BGB). On application, and with the child's consent, the court may allow the child to bear a hyphenated name made up of the old and new family names (in either order) if the child's welfare so requires (§ 1757 III 1 No. 2 BGB). On application, and with the child's consent, the court may also change the child's first name or add a new first name or names if this is consistent with the child's welfare (§ 1757 I 1 No. 1 BGB).

3   Setting Aside an Adoption Decree

As a rule, an adoption decree, once made, is final and irrevocable. The idea is to provide a stable legal basis for the new family. Under *exceptional circumstances* set out in the Civil Code, however, the law departs from this principle and permits a revocation:

This is the case where

- the applications or consents required for an adoption were not (validly) given or there was a *fundamental mistake or other serious flaw* (a mistake as to the child's identity, duress, etc.) in making the declaration (§ 1760 BGB). Any such defect, however, is purged three years after the effective date of the adoption order (§ 1762 II 1 BGB). Even before then, there is a ban on revocation if the revocation would seriously jeopardize the child's welfare and there is no overriding interest on the part of the adoptive parent(s) (§ 1761 II BGB). A missing consent is irrelevant if the requirements for replacing the consent in question are present at the time of either the adoption or the revocation proceedings (§ 1761 I BGB);

- the family court considers revocation necessary *to protect the child* (§ 1763 I BGB). As the wording of § 1763 BGB makes clear, this exception applies only as long as the child is still a minor. Once the child has reached adulthood, the adoption order can no longer be revoked pursuant to § 1763 BGB, even in cases of serious abuse by the adoptive parent(s).[30]

The revocation of an adoption decree does not have retroactive effect (§ 1764 I 1 BGB). Once the revocation order has become absolute, the family ties previously established come to an end and those previously severed revive (§ 1764 II, III BGB). The natural parents do not automatically regain parental responsibility. However, an application for parental responsibility would normally be granted unless it is contrary to the child's best interests (§ 1764 IV BGB).

---

30   BGH, NJW (2014): 1663.

4   The Right to Know One's Genetic Origins and Adoptees

Ideas about the 'protective effects' of not knowing one's genetic origins (where they point to persons other than one's legal parents) have not been validated empirically. Quite the contrary: research indicates that children who learn, early on, that they are not the biological children of their legal parents have an easier time adjusting to and incorporating that aspect of their identity.[31]

In 1989, the *German Constitutional Court* recognized that the *right to know one's genetic origins is an integral part of the personality right protected by the German Constitution, arts 21 and 1*.[32] According to the Constitutional Court, developing one's individual identity is intimately connected with knowledge of the elements that constitute it. Among these constitutive elements are one's genetic origins. A person's genetic origins do not just determine that person's genetic make-up. They also hold a central place in an individual's consciousness and influence his or her personal development and self-perception.[33] While the Constitutional Court has recognized the right, the right is *not absolute*: for a start, it does not give a right to obtain information not previously available, but only a right not to have available information withheld.[34] Secondly, the right has to be balanced against possible countervailing rights of other persons, and in particular the privacy rights of the legal or genetic parents.[35]

Like all constitutional rights, the right to know one's genetic origins is, in the first instance, a *right against the state*. It requires the state to abstain from measures violating the right to know one's genetic origins. In an appropriate case, the right may also impose a duty on the state to take positive steps, through its legislature or courts, to make the right enforceable as between private parties. The state does not infringe the right to know one's genetic origins if its action or inaction is suitable, necessary, and proportionate to protect a countervailing right or interest.[36]

The right to know one's genetic origins is *particularly relevant for adoptees* and for children born of assisted reproduction with donor sperm (on the right to information of the latter group, see *infra* Part 2, chapter 5). Research on adoptees has shown that adopted children benefit from being able to talk about the fact of being adopted and about their birth parents with their

---

31   Heinz Kindler et al., "Kenntnis der Abstammung bei fragmentierter Elternschaft aus humanwissenschaftlicher Sicht," NZFam (2017): 929.

32   BVerfG, NJW (1989): 891.

33   BVerfG, NJW (1989): 891.

34   BVerfG, NJW (1989): 891.

35   BVerfG, NJW (1989): 891, 892.

36   BVerfG, NJW (1989): 891, 892.

adoptive families, particularly if the relationship with the adoptive family is generally a good one.[37]

§ 9b II 1 of the *Adoptionsvermittlungsgesetz* ('AdVermiG'; in English: 'Adoption Placement Act') accordingly gives the adoptee's legal representative, and, once the adoptee has reached the age of sixteen years, the adoptee him- or herself, a *right to inspect the adoption files*. The right covers only information pertaining to the adoptee's own origins or life history (for instance, the circumstances surrounding the adoptee's birth and adoption; whether there were any biological siblings at the time of the adoption; and the profession, origins, and general life circumstances of the adoptee's biological family, but only up until the time of the adoption order).[38] Exceptionally, additional information may be covered if the adoptee can show a legitimate interest: this generally requires a legally protected interest, such as an intention to pursue a damages, inheritance, or maintenance claim,[39] to check the genetic disposition for an illness or to obtain a bone marrow transplant. According to some courts, coming to terms with a troubled relationship with one's adoptive parents may also constitute a legitimate interest.[40] Whether the intention to contact one's biological relatives in an attempt to get 'first-hand' knowledge of the adoption decision constitutes a legitimate interest is still an open question. As the law now stands, the answer is probably no, since the legislature has opted for a right to inspect the files, rather than a right to personal contact and communication. Mere curiosity is certainly not enough.[41] The right is excluded under § 9b II 2 AdVermiG by the overriding rights of another interested party—in particular, the birth parents. The Constitutional Court has stressed that the birth mother, in particular, has a right to keep her sexual contacts private and that requiring her to disclose them constitutes a serious infringement of her personality right, which can be justified only by an even more significant informational interest on the part of the child.[42]

§ 9b II AdVermiG grants only a right to inspect the files of German adoption agencies. In international adoptions, the relevant data may be stored with adoption agencies abroad. Access to *foreign files* is generally governed by the law of the state in question. The Hague Convention on Protection of Children and Co-operation in respect of Intercountry Adoption (or 'Hague Adoption

---

37   Kindler et al., "Kenntnis der Abstammung bei fragmentierter Elternschaft aus humanwissenschaftlicher Sicht," 931.

38   Jörg Reinhardt, *Adoptionsvermittlungsgesetz*, 4th online ed. (2017), § 9b para. 9.

39   LG Münster, NJW (1999): 726.

40   LG Bremen, NJW (1999): 729.

41   Reinhardt, *Adoptionsvermittlungsgesetz*, § 9b para. 10.

42   BVerfG – 1 BvR 472/14 = NJW (2015): 1506.

Convention') does not impose an obligation on all contracting states to ensure access to its stored data. Article 30 II of the Convention requires them only to ensure access to such information "as is permitted by the law of that State." For signatories to the European Convention on the Adoption of Children, however, access to the files is required by article 22 III of that Convention. As in German law, regard is to be had to the circumstances and the respective rights of the child and his or her parents of origin. The European Court of Human Rights ('ECtHR') has held that withholding information about a person's genetic origins is an infringement of the personality right guaranteed by the European Convention on Human Rights ('ECHR'), art .8 .[43] It follows that, for European Union ('EU') member states, access to the relevant data (subject to a balancing test) has to be ensured, even if the state in question has not (yet) ratified the European Adoption Convention.

3   *Controversial Issues and Proposals for Reform*
1   Adoptions of Adults

While the numbers of adoptions of minors are steadily declining (owing to the lower birth rate, the improved status of single parents, and competition from modern reproductive technologies), adult adoptions are on the increase. According to a survey conducted by the head organization of Germany's registry officers, the percentage of adult adoptions has gone up from 16.3 percent in 1986 to 47.3 percent in 2006, and it continues to rise.[44]

Although the adoption of minors has constituted the central case of adoption since 1961, adult adoptions continue to be possible if they are "morally justified" (§ 1767 BGB). They owe their popularity to two legal consequences of creating a parent–child relationship: first, the change in the adoptee's name to that of the adoptive parent (§§ 1767 II, 1754 BGB). This is important because, according to German law, a name change can generally be brought about only by marriage or a successful application under the—very restrictive—*Namensänderungsgesetz* (Name Change Act). Secondly, tax benefits: an adoption puts the adoptee into a more favorable gift and inheritance tax bracket with higher exempt amounts and lower tax rates (§ 15 I No. 2 *Erbschaftssteuergesetz* (Inheritance Tax Act, 'ErbStG').

---

43 ECtHR, FamRZ (2012): 1935.

44 Tobias Helms and Andreas Botthof, "Die Volljährigenadoption als Mittel der Nachlassplanung—Plädoyer für die Einschränkung eines anachronistischen Rechtsinstituts," in *Zivilrecht und Steuerrecht, Erwerb von Todes wegen und Schenkung: Festschrift für Jens Peter Meincke zum 80. Geburtstag*, ed. Karlheinz Muscheler and Reinhard Zimmermann (München: Beck, 2015), 148.

While adult adoptions for the sole or main purpose of changing one's name or getting a tax break are not morally justified, and hence legally impermissible, there is a real danger that cases of abuse may go undetected. After all, courts are largely dependent on what the parties tell them about their motives for seeking an adoption, and the indications are that adult adoptions are rarely refused.[45]

Hence, there are proposals to restrict the availability of adult adoptions (in line with other European countries) or even to outlaw them altogether, since there is no real need for them.[46] An alternative might be to reduce the incentive to abuse by removing the beneficial name and tax consequences of adult adoptions. The tax benefits for adopted children were introduced in 1923 to promote the adoption of orphaned minors.[47] Differentiating between minor and adult adoptees for gift and inheritance tax purposes (as France does, for instance) would thus be a viable (and, in particular, a constitutionally permissible) option.[48]

2   Adoptions by Same-Sex Partners

As we saw above, persons who are not married to each other may generally only adopt alone (§ 1741 II 1 BGB). Since 2005, registered partners have been able to adopt the biological child of their partner.[49] In 2014, following a decision by the German Constitutional Court,[50] it was expressly provided that a registered partner may also adopt the adopted child of his or her partner.[51] However, simultaneous joint adoptions by registered partners remained an impossibility. This hot topic was unexpectedly resolved in the fall of 2017. As a result of the Same-Sex Marriage Act of July 20, 2017,[52] it has become possible for same-sex couples to get married. If they do so, they come within § 1741 II 2 BGB—that is, they can only adopt jointly.

---

45   Rainer Frank, "Brauchen wir Adoption," FamRZ (2007): 1693, 1694.
46   Frank, "Brauchen wir Adoption," 1694; Helms and Botthof, "Die Volljährigenadoption als Mittel der Nachlassplanung," 161.
47   Frank-Werner Krause, "Die Volljährigenadoption: Probleme der Adoption Erwachsener und deren Lösung de lege lata und de lega ferenda" (diss., University of Freiburg, 1971), 25, 118.
48   Helms and Botthof, "Die Volljährigenadoption als Mittel der Nachlassplanung," 158–60.
49   *Lebenspartnerschaftsgesetz* (Registered Partnership Act) in connection with § 1754 I, III BGB.
50   BVerfG, NJW (2013): 847.
51   BGBl. 2014 I, 786.
52   BGBl. 2017 I, 2787.

unmarried	registered partners & same-sex married couples
• may only adopt alone	• may adopt the biological child of their partner (since 2005) • may adopt the adopted child of their partner (since 2014) • may adopt jointly (since 2017)

FIGURE 4   Illustration by author

3   In-Family Adoptions

In quantitative terms, the reality of adoption has moved away from outside adoptions by non-family members. Most adoptions of minors today are in-family adoptions. In 2014, 60.8 percent of minors were adopted by a stepparent or relatives. Approximately two decades earlier (in 1992), in-family adoptions had accounted for only 52.8 percent of the total number of adoptions.[53]

Because of the high divorce rate and the high number of extramarital relationships, more than half of all adoptions today are by *stepparents*. Stepparent adoptions are often considered to be in a child's best interests because they vest a de facto familial relationship with the legal form desired by the parties. They are currently favored by the law. However, they are more problematic than appears at first sight. The aim of a stepparent adoption is usually to 'exclude' the outside parent for good. Accordingly, both the Constitutional Court and the Supreme Court have stressed that more stringent conditions apply for replacing the outside parent's consent pursuant to § 1748 BGB than in third-party adoptions.[54]

The danger of stepparent adoptions consists in the fact that they create a lifelong parent–child relationship irrespective of the fate of the stepparent's marriage. Even if the marriage fails a few years down the line, the stepparent adoption stands. The stepparent continues to be liable for child support and the child continues to be eligible for a forced share of the stepparent's estate. In the past, a number of stepparents have (unsuccessfully) tried to reverse the adoption decree after their marriage to the child's biological parent ended.[55] Stepchildren are often (perhaps even usually) adopted as a favor to the parent-spouse.

---

53   Statistisches Bundesamt, *Statistiken der Kinder- und Jugendhilfe: Adoptionen* (2015), 5, 23.
54   BVerfG, NJW (2006): 827; BGH, FamRZ (2005): 891.
55   BGH, FamRZ (1971): 89; BayObLG, FamRZ (2000): 768.

At the time of the adoption, the possibility of divorce is not considered (or, at any rate, is tactfully not talked about).

The problem of stepparent adoptions might be addressed in different ways. One option (and incidentally one with which the Netherlands experimented a while back[56]) would be to outlaw them altogether. Another might be to try to ensure that they are well considered, by requiring, for instance, that the stepparent be married to the child's biological parent for a minimum number of years before an adoption can be granted. Finally, the legal consequences of stepparent adoptions could be curtailed. In France, for example, an *adoption plénière*, which dissolves the child's legal ties with his or her family of birth, is available only exceptionally, where the adoption is by a stepparent (Code Civil, art. 345-1). A further option might be to remove the need for an adoption altogether by granting stepparents more legal rights with respect to their stepchildren (for instance, joint custody rights).[57]

In addition to stepparent adoptions, the current law also allows adoptions by grandparents, siblings, aunts, uncles, and other *close relatives*. The only requirement is that the adoption (as any adoption) benefits the child and that it is likely that a parent–child relationship will develop between the parties (§ 1741 I 1 BGB). Adoptions by relatives are not uncommon. They are problematic, however, insofar as they superimpose fictitious legal relationships on natural ones. They can turn biological grandparents into parents, a mother into a sister, or siblings into nephews and nieces. If the child is adopted by a relative while the biological parents are still alive, the child may be acutely aware of these idiosyncracies. German adoption agencies accordingly have reservations about adoptions by relatives, and recommend them only where the alternatives seem clearly inferior for the child.[58] Especially where the parties are closely related, a foster relationship will often be preferable. On the other hand, the objections to adoptions by relatives diminish as the biological ties between the prospective adoptive parent and the adoptee become more tenuous.

4   (Semi-)Open and Closed Adoptions

As a result of the dissemination of Anglo-American adoption research, there is now a consensus in the social sciences that incognito adoptions may not always be in the best interests of the child. Also, the German Constitutional

---

56   Frank, "Brauchen wir Adoption," 1695.

57   Tobias Helms, "Rechtliche, biologische und soziale Elternschaft—Herausforderung durch neue Familienformen," NJW-Beilage (2016): 49, 52.

58   Bundesarbeitsgemeinschaft der Landesjugendämter, *Empfehlungen zur Adoptionsvermittlung*, 7th ed. (2014), para. 7.1.3.

Court recognizes a right of adoptees to know their genetic origins (see *supra* paragraph 2.4), meaning that a de facto link between the child and his or her birth family may well be maintained even after an adoption decree is issued.

If adoption research is correct in suggesting that adoptees find it hard to come to terms with their origins, then a more open form of adoption may well be appropriate, especially (but not only) for older children or children who are adopted by stepparents. Open or semi-open adoptions are increasingly being practiced. The term 'open adoption' describes the sociological reality that, in this form of adoption, the adoptive parents agree to waive their right to ano-nymity (§ 1758 BGB) to some extent.[59] In a 'semi-open adoption,' on the other hand, the birth parents do not meet the adoptive parents (whose anonymity is generally not compromised) nor are they meant to have post-adoption contact with the child. Rather, the idea is to provide them with information (photos, videos, etc.) about the child and the child's development. Generally, however, the term '(semi-)open adoption' is a collective term, which is not limited to certain types of post-adoption relationship, but encompasses all adoptions in which, in the interests of the child, some kind of de facto relationship between the child and the birth family is maintained.

Since the principle of full adoption leads to a severance of the *legal* ties be-tween the birth parents and the adopted child (§§ 1754, 1755 BGB), however, an open or semi-open adoption can currently be established and conducted only on a voluntary basis—that is, it is a matter for the discretion of the adop-tive parent(s) whether the promised openness is in fact adhered to. The future of (semi-)open adoptions might well include (more) legally enforceable rights for the biological parents. However, a mere four decades after the enactment of the Adoption Act of 1976, which brought the change to full adoption, it may be too much to expect another paradigm shift from the legislature, without strong outside prompting, at least. At this point, there would seem to be a consensus that more social science research is needed before the time is ripe for legisla-tive change. The impetus for changes in the current law will thus have to come from the social sciences, and, in particular, from the findings of psychology.

Which consequences (if any) for the future of the law of adoption can be derived from these social science findings, and whether open adoptions should become available even against the wishes of the adoptive parents, are also constitutional questions. What is clear is that any future legal rule would have to be sufficiently elastic and malleable to allow a measured and 'tailored'

---

59   Angela von Schlieffen, "Offene Adoptionen—Ein Grund zur Reform des Adoptionsrechts" (diss., University of Berlin, 1996), 38 et seq.

response appropriate to the highly individualized needs and circumstances of the different parties involved in the adoption triangle.

5   Adoptions by Lesbian Co-Mothers

While adoption is an ancient institution, it has relatively recently acquired a new area of application: an adoption order is needed as a regular supplement where assisted reproductive technologies are carried out on lesbian couples. This is because of the current state of the German law of descent and parentage, which defines the legal mother (§ 1591 BGB) and the legal father (§ 1592 BGB) of a child. Where two lesbian women decide to have a child with donor sperm, the partner giving birth will be the child's legal mother, pursuant to § 1591 BGB. However, the other woman cannot establish her intended co-motherhood according to any of the three methods (marriage to the mother; voluntary acknowledgment of parentage; or court finding of genetic parentage) set out in § 1592 BGB. This is because § 1592 BGB opens with the words: "The father of a child is the man who". This wording clearly does not fit the case of the lesbian co-mother. Hence, she is forced to fall back on adoption. A stepparent adoption—which would give her joint parental status alongside the child's birth mother (§ 1754 I BGB)—is available to her if she is either married to (§ 1741 II 3 BGB) or lives in a registered partnership with (§ 9 VII *Lebenspartnerschaftsgesetz* (Registered Partners' Act, 'LPartG') the child's birth mother. However, adoption is a complicated and protracted procedure, involving, as it does, a 'best interests' test (§ 1741 I 1 BGB) and a home study (§ 1744 BGB). Recently, some first-instance courts have indicated that they might be prepared to waive the latter requirement where the child is by an anonymous sperm donor.[60] While this is a welcome move, it clearly does not overcome all the objections (especially from an equality point of view) that attach to an adoption solution for a lesbian intended co-mother. Moreover, an adoption is not a viable option if the intended co-mother is not a spouse or registered partner, but a mere cohabitant. Cohabitants can only adopt alone, meaning that the adoption would end the parental status of the child's birth mother. This, however, is almost never the desired outcome.

The solution, in my opinion, does not lie in changes to the law of adoption for intending co-mothers. Rather, the law of descent and parentage should be modernized. The *Arbeitskreis Abstammungsrecht* (a working group on the German law of descent and parentage) recommended in 2017 that a lesbian intended co-mother should be in the same position as a man who wants to be

---

60   AG Elmshorn, NJW (2011): 1085, 1986; AG Göttingen, FamRZ (2015): 1982, 1983.

recognized as the legal father of a child. According to the working group's recommendations, the lesbian partner would be the child's legal mother (according to a modified version of § 1592 BGB) if she is *either* married to or living in a registered partnership with the birth mother at the time of the child's birth *or* files an acknowledgment of her co-motherhood *or* is adjudged to be the child's co-mother by a court of law (with the court looking to her consent to the artificial insemination, rather than any genetic link in reaching its finding). The working group wants to limit the third option to medically assisted insemination procedures:[61] an abridgement of the proposed reform with which I, for one, do not agree. The only question should be whether there was unequivocal pre-insemination consent.

Part 2: Assisted Reproduction

1 *A Partial Legal Framework*

In Germany, as elsewhere, assisted reproduction is a boom business. In 2015, 20,949 children were born with the aid of assisted reproductive services, which is one thousand more than in the year before.[62] Approximately one thousand children per year are born as a result of insemination by donor.[63] According to a recent estimate, up to 100,000 children who were born as a result of sperm donation live in Germany today.[64] Despite the practical importance of assisted reproduction, and despite longstanding criticism, the legal framework remains patchy. To date, there is *no comprehensive Assisted Reproduction Act* or unified legislative response. Rather, various statutes, and in particular two public law ones—the *Embryo Protection Act* (*Embryonenschutzgesetz* or 'ESchG') and the *Adoption Placement Act* (*Adoptionsvermittlungsgesetz* or 'AdVermiG')—deal with certain forms of assisted reproductive services, by outlawing and punishing them. Much is left to the *self-regulation of the medical community*. The German BGB contains but two provisions that specifically reference assisted reproduction, and both are fairly recent additions to the Civil Code. The second one was inserted as recently as July 2018.

---

61   Arbeitskreis Abstammungsrecht, *Abschlussbericht* (Köln: Bundesanzeiger Verlag, 2017), 70.

62   Deutsches IVF Register, *Jahrbuch 2016*, 8.

63   Nina Dethloff and Rudolf Gerhardt, "Ein Reproduktionsmedizingesetz ist überfällig: Zuordnung des Kindes zu den Wuscheltern nicht zum Samenspender," ZRP (2013): 91, 93.

64   MünchKomm/*Wellenhofer*, 7th ed. (2017), § 1600 para. 53.

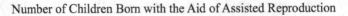

Number of Children Born with the Aid of Assisted Reproduction

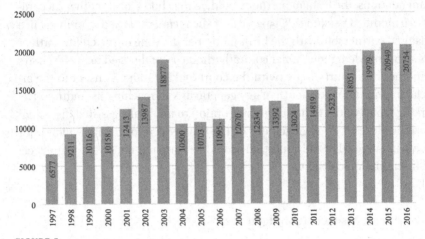

FIGURE 5

SOURCE: DEUTSCHES IVF REGISTER, *JAHRBUCH 2017*, 43

The first provision is *§ 1600 IV BGB*. It deals with the persons entitled to contest the paternity of a child. It reads:

> If the child, with the consent of the man and the mother was conceived by means of artificial insemination by sperm donation from a third person, the contestation of paternity by the man or the mother is excluded.

The obvious purpose of the section is to exclude paternity challenges by the persons who, at the time of the conception, intended to be the parents of the resulting child. The section was inserted into the Civil Code in 2002.[65] Before its insertion, it was highly controversial whether a man who had consented to the donor insemination of his partner could contest his paternity of the resulting child. If the man was married to the mother at the time of the child's birth, his legal status as father followed from § 1592 No. 1 BGB, which attaches a prima facie paternity to the fact that the man was married to the child's mother at the time of the child's birth. While there was a body of academic opinion that argued that a paternity contest in this situation would be in bad faith and consequently should be excluded,[66] the German Supreme Court was of the opinion that such a contest remained possible within the

---

65   *Kinderrechteverbesserungsgesetz* of April 9, 2002, BGBl. 2002 I, 1239.

66   Franz Harder, "Wer sind Vater und Mutter?," JuS, 1986, 505, 507; Andreas Roth, "Die Zustimmung eines Mannes zur heterologen Insemination seiner Ehefrau," FamRZ (1996): 769, 771; Nina Dethloff, "Reform des Kindschaftsrechts," NJW (1992): 2200, 2207.

time limits established by law.[67] However, the Supreme Court penalized this change of heart by finding that consent to the insemination implied a contractual undertaking to provide financial support for the resulting child.[68] With the insertion of § 1600 IV BGB, the situation was clarified in favor of an exclusion of the right to contest paternity for both the mother and the man who consents to her donor insemination.

The second provision is the newly inserted *§ 1600d IV BGB*, which has been in force only since July 1, 2018. It reads:

> If the child was born as a result of a medically assisted artificial insemination procedure in a medical facility within the meaning of § 1a No. 9 of the Transplantation Act with sperm donated by a third party to a facility within the meaning of § 2 I 1 of the Sperm Donors' Register Act, the sperm donor cannot be adjudicated to be the father of the child.

The aim of the provision is to protect sperm donors from paternity suits by their genetic offspring, but only on the twin conditions that the insemination by donor be (1) medically assisted and (2) with sperm officially donated to a specified facility.

There is one more provision in the Civil Code, which does not mention assisted reproduction in its actual phraseology, but which was inserted as a direct reaction to the new medical technology: *§ 1591 BGB*. This provides that the mother of a child is the woman who gives birth. The presence or absence of a genetic link to the child does not play a role, and the legal maternity of the birth mother can be neither contested nor otherwise revised (short of adoption). The express aim of the section, which was inserted by the Children's Law Reform Act of December 16, 1997,[69] was to discourage surrogate motherhood. In Germany, as will be discussed in more detail below, surrogacy is prohibited by two public law statutes—the Embryo Protection Act and the Adoption Placement Act—but it was deemed advisable to insert § 1591 BGB nonetheless.[70]

---

67   BGH, NJW (1995): 2028; 1995, 2921; 1983, 2073.
68   BGH, NJW (1995): 2928.
69   BGBl. I, 2942.
70   RegE, BT-Drucks. 13/4899, 82; BR-Drucks. 180/96, 61, 92; MünchKomm/*Wellenhofer*, 7th ed. (2017), § 1591 para. 1.

2 *Permissible and Impermissible Forms*

There is no German statute that deals specifically with assisted reproduction. The central act is a criminal statute: the *Embryonenschutzgesetz* ('ESchG') or Embryo Protection Act, which has been in force since January 1, 1991.[71] This Act criminalizes certain assisted reproduction practices. It is supplemented by the *Adoptionsvermittlungsgesetz* ('AdVermiG') or Adoption Placement Act, which also outlaws or punishes certain forms of assisted reproductive services.

For our purposes, the following prohibitions contained in the Embryo Protection Act are relevant:

– transferring the unfertilized egg of one woman to another woman (§ 1 I No. 1 ESchG);
– fertilizing an egg with the intention of causing the pregnancy of a woman other than the woman who provided the egg (§ 1 I No. 2, II ESchG);
– artificially inseminating or transferring a human embryo to a woman who is prepared permanently to place the resulting child with a third party upon birth (surrogate) (§ 1 I No. 7 ESchG);
– fertilizing an egg without the consent of the woman and the man whose gametes are used (§ 4 I No. 1 ESchG);
– transferring an embryo to a woman without her consent (§ 4 I No. 2 ESchG);
– knowingly fertilizing an egg with the sperm of a man after his death (§ 4 II ESchG);
– cloning a human being (§ 6 ESchG).

The woman who provides the egg or embryo and the woman to whom the egg or embryo is transferred, as well as the surrogate and the person who wants to bring up the child in the surrogate's stead, are exempt from criminal liability (§ 1 III Nos. 1, 2 ESchG). The same goes for the woman whose egg is fertilized with the sperm of a man after his death (§ 4 III ESchG).

According to the Embryo Protection Act, only a medical professional may carry out an artificial insemination procedure or transfer an embryo to a woman (§ 9 Nos. 1, 3 ESchG). Non-compliance with § 9 Nos. 1 and 3 ESchG is a criminal offense (§ 11 I Nos. 1, 3 ESchG). However, a woman who performs an artificial insemination on herself and the man who provides the sperm for it are exempt from liability (§ 11 II ESchG).

---

71   BGBl. I, 2746.

Also relevant for our purposes are the following provisions of the Adoption Placement Act:

- it is prohibited to cause a pregnant woman, who has her residence or habitual domicile in Germany, to give up her child for adoption or to assist her in doing so by providing her, in a businesslike manner, with an opportunity for giving birth abroad (§ 5 III AdVermiG);
- it is prohibited to engage in placement activities directed at a third party taking in a child on a permanent basis, and in particular by means of a man's acknowledgment of paternity of a child who is not genetically his own (§ 5 IV AdVermiG);
- it is prohibited to procure a surrogate mother for intending parents and vice versa (§ 13c AdVermiG).

Non-compliance with § 5 III AdVermiG is subject to a fine (§ 14 II No. 2 AdVermiG); non-compliance with § 13c AdVermiG is a criminal offense (§ 14b AdVermiG).

Although they do not attach criminal sanctions to the relevant behavior in all instances, the Embryo Protection Act and the Adoption Placement Act clearly denounce egg donation and surrogate motherhood. Hence, both egg donation and surrogacy must be considered impermissible reproductive practices according to German law. A national policy against surrogate motherhood is also implicit in § 1591 BGB ("The mother of a child is the woman who gives birth to it"), which was inserted into the BGB by the Children's Law Reform Act of December 16, 1997[72] with the express aim of discouraging surrogate motherhood.

On the other hand, the logical inference from the detailed prohibitions of the Embryo Protection Act is that everything that is not expressly forbidden by the Act is allowed. In particular, the Embryo Protection Act does not prohibit artificial insemination as such, although it requires that it be carried out by a doctor. As a result, both insemination by husband or steady partner (*homologe Insemination*) and insemination by donor (*heterologe Insemination*) are allowed. The use of anonymous sperm in donor insemination and the use of sperm cocktails are not expressly prohibited, either. However, these practices are incompatible with the constitutionally protected right to know one's genetic origins.[73] A guideline by the Federal Medical Council of Germany (*Bundesärztekammer*) provides that doctors engaged in assisted reproduction with donor sperm have to document the identity of the donor and the waiver

---

72   BGBl. I, 2942.
73   For this right and its constitutional protection, see *infra* chap. 5.

of the right to anonymity on the part of both the donor and the intending parents.[74]

Moreover, in practice, even procedures that the Embryo Protection Act attempts to outlaw occur. The German medical profession can generally be relied upon to observe the Act's provisions. Accordingly, prohibited artificial insemination procedures that require medical assistance (such as egg donation) hardly happen. Not all insemination procedures that the Embryo Protection Act prohibits require medical assistance, however. The use of a surrogate mother to bear children for couples who are unable to conceive for themselves, for instance, is a process that is thousands of years old—just think of the biblical story of Abraham and his infertile wife Sarah. Whereas the form of surrogate motherhood in which the carrier is not genetically related to the child (generally known as 'full' or 'gestational' surrogacy), is dependent on the advances of modern medicine, the simpler form, in which the surrogate mother is also the child's genetic mother ('partial' or 'traditional' surrogacy), is not. Artificial insemination procedures, whether in the context of surrogacy or on a woman who intends to raise the child herself, can be performed quite simply in the privacy of one's home, on a 'do-it-yourself' basis.

All the indications are that they are so performed frequently. German notaries report being consulted by an increasing number of single women, as well as hetero- and homosexual couples, who express a wish to 'regularize' the legal consequences of a private insemination procedure in a notarized 'parentage contract.'[75] Model forms for such contracts exist.[76] Issues concerning the parentage of children created through private insemination procedures—commonly referred to as 'Becherspenden' or, in English, 'sperm in a cup'—have occupied the German courts on a number of occasions.[77]

3   Access to Assisted Reproductive Services

In Germany, as has been seen, artificial reproduction is not heavily regulated by statute.[78] Moreover, the statutory law in question prohibits only certain artificial insemination procedures, but says nothing about who has access to the legally permissible ones. Where the procedure in question does not require

---

74   (*Muster-*)*Richtlinie zur Durchführung der Assistierten Reproduktion* of February 17, 2006, para. 5.3.3.2; Richtlinie zur Entnahme und Übertragung von menschlichen Keimzellen im Rahmen der assistierten Reproduktion of October 6, 2017, paras. 2.1.1.6, 2.2.3.

75   For a fuller discussion of parentage contracts, see *infra* chap. 7.

76   See, e.g., Bergschneider/*Grziwotz*, *Beck'sches Formularhandbuch Familienrecht*, 5th ed. (2017), form 5.

77   To select just a few of the recent cases: BGH, NJW (2017): 3379; 2015, 1820; 2013, 2589; OLG Bamberg, RNotZ (2017): 538.

78   See *supra* chap. 2.

medical assistance (such as in vivo fertilization using 'sperm in a cup'), access is completely unregulated. On the other hand, where the procedure requires medical assistance (such as in vitro fertilization, for example), access is governed by professional self-regulation. Currently, this self-regulation takes the form of various *Richtlinien zur Durchführung der Assistierten Reproduktion* (guidelines on assisted reproduction issued by the Medical Boards of the various German states (*Landesärztekammern*)). In the main, these guidelines adopt the provisions of the *Musterrichtlinie zur Durchführung der Assistierten Reproduktion*—a model guideline on assisted reproduction that was issued by the Federal Medical Council of Germany (*Bundesärztekammer*) in 2006 and significantly revised in 2017.

The declared aim of the 2006 *Musterrichtlinie* was to provide guidance for medical professionals involved in assisted reproduction.[79] In addition to defining terms and setting out the conditions that have to be met in order for a particular assisted reproductive procedure to be medically indicated, it contained general conditions of access (*Allgemeine Zulassungbedingungen*).[80] These provisions were easily the most controversial in the entire guideline. The new 2017 guideline, on the other hand, limits itself to medical questions and deliberately refrains from commenting on the socio-political ramifications of assisted reproduction. It is currently unclear, therefore, to what extent medical professionals are still guided by the conditions of access set out in the 2006 guideline.

Contents of the 2017 *Richtlinie*[81]
1   Introduction to the subject and legal bases
    1.1   Legal framework, authorization, effect and background
    1.2   Scope of application
    1.3   Legal basis for removal and transmission of human germ cells in the context of assisted reproduction
    1.4   Definitions
2   Requirements for the removal and transmission of human germ cells
    2.1   Legal requirements for information and education before removal and transfer human germ cells
    2.2   Statements on the content of information and education required from a medical point of view

---

79   (*Muster-*)*Richtlinie zur Durchführung der Assistierten Reproduktion* of February 17, 2006, preface.
80   (*Muster-*)*Richtlinie zur Durchführung der Assistierten Reproduktion* of February 17, 2006, para. 3.
81   (*Muster-*)*Richtlinie zur Durchführung der Assistierten Reproduktion* of October 10, 2017.

According to paragraph 3.1.1. of the 2006 *Musterrichtlinie*, assisted reproduction is generally reserved to married couples, and generally requires that the husband's sperm be used. Assisted reproductive services may also be provided to an unmarried woman, but only if the doctor treating her is convinced that the woman has a permanent male partner who is ready to acknowledge paternity of the resulting child. Donor sperm may be used if insemination by husband or permanent male partner has been unsuccessful or is not medically feasible to start with.[82]

These restrictive conditions of access excluded unmarried women without a steady male partner, as well as women living in lesbian (registered) partnerships or even lesbian marriages (same-sex marriage having been possible in Germany since October 1, 2017). Single men and male homosexual partners or married couples are excluded as well. However, their exclusion is justified, since they would have to rely on assisted reproductive procedures—namely, surrogacy and possibly egg donation, which are currently outlawed by the Embryo Protection Act. The 2006 *Musterrichtlinie* justifies its exclusion of single women and lesbian couples by pointing to the child's need for a social and legal father.[83]

The exclusion of lesbian couples and, in my opinion, also the exclusion of single women from the full panoply of permissible assisted reproductive procedures is outdated and unjustified. Since 2014, following a decision by the German Constitutional Court,[84] registered partners have been able to adopt the adopted child of their partners.[85] And as a result of the Same-Sex Marriage Act of July 20, 2017,[86] same-sex married couples are placed on the same footing, as far as adoptions are concerned, as heterosexual married couples (that is, they can adopt only jointly (§ 1741 II 2 BGB)). This development is in line with an overwhelming body of expert evidence to suggest that reservations about children growing up with gay or lesbian parents are unfounded.[87] Given this approach to the adoption of children by gays and lesbians, it cannot be right that lesbian couples are denied access to an alternative and, in the eyes

---

82   (*Muster-*)*Richtlinie zur Durchführung der Assistierten Reproduktion* of February 17, 2006, para. 5.3.1.

83   (*Muster-*)*Richtlinie zur Durchführung der Assistierten Reproduktion* of February 17, 2006, para 3.1.1.

84   BVerfG, NJW (2013): 847.

85   BGBl. 2014 I, 786.

86   BGBl. 2017 I, 2787.

87   BVerfG, NJW (2013): 847, 852. The Legal Committee of the German *Bundestag* has also made it clear that, in excluding registered partners from joint adoptions, it did not intend to cast doubt on the parenting abilities of gays and lesbians (BT-Drucks. 14/4550, 6).

of some intending parents, superior (because of the possible genetic link with the child) non-coital route to parenthood. The exclusion of single women is also unjustified: while, in an ideal world, any child should grow up with two (loving) parents, single parenthood is in fact widespread. Today, 20 percent of German parents raise their children alone. Expressed in numbers, that is 1.5 million women and 157,000 men.[88]

While there may be an outside legal parent (responsible for child support, etc.), this need not be the case. The other parent may be deceased, for example, or his parental status may never have been established (by acknowledgment of paternity or court order). Moreover, there is research to indicate that the children of single parents do well. They do not receive less care and attention than the children of two-parent homes, and they generally grow up under satisfactory conditions for their health and welfare.[89] As the German Constitutional Court has found, what is problematic is not being raised by *fewer* than two parents, but being raised by *more* than two: multiple parents present a danger of conflicting roles, disputes over respective areas of authority, and divided loyalties.[90] Single parenthood does not present these dangers, nor can any other valid objections be raised against it, as is amply evidenced by the fact that single persons, including those of a gay or lesbian orientation, are eligible to adopt (§ 1741 II 1 BGB).

The above view seems to be shared by at least some members of the German medical profession. Despite the provisions of the 2006 *Musterrichtlinie*, there are and always have been fertility clinics that perform inseminations with donor sperm on lesbians and single women. Interestingly, however, it seems to have become established practice, where single women are concerned, to make medical assistance conditional on the woman providing a 'guarantor' who agrees to pay child support and to absolve the sperm donor from any support obligations. Frequently, it is the woman's parents who act as guarantors. Despite the (welcome) willingness of some medical professionals to break ranks and to ignore the 2006 *Musterrichtlinie*'s outdated provisions, the current state of the law is clearly unsatisfactory. Access to a service that is so important, from the point of view of fundamental rights, as assisted reproduction should not be allowed to depend on professional self-regulation. It should be restricted by statute, if it is to be restricted at all.

88   Bundesministerium für Familie, Senioren, Frauen und Jugend, *Alleinerziehende in Deutschland—Lebenssituationen und Lebenswirklichkeiten von Müttern und Kindern*, 28th ed., 5, https://wir-sind-alleinerziehend.de/alleinerziehende-in-deutschland/ (last accessed June 25, 2018).

89   Bundesministerium für Familie, Senioren, Frauen und Jugend, *Alleinerziehende in Deutschland*, 21.

90   BVerfG, NJW (2003): 2151, 2153.

4   *The Allocation of Parental Status*

As the law currently stands, the allocation of parental status for children of assisted reproduction follows the ordinary rules. These are set out in §§ 1591 et seq. BGB:

The *legal mother of the child* is the woman who gave birth to it. If the provisions of the Embryo Protection Act—namely, the Act's ban on egg donation and on surrogate motherhood—are complied with, the birth mother will also be the child's genetic mother and intended social mother. Even if the birth mother is not the child's genetic mother (egg donation) or not the woman who intends to raise the child as her own (surrogacy), her status as the child's legal mother can be neither prevented nor challenged. It can be terminated only by an adoption order (§ 1755 I 1 BGB).

When it comes to the *child's second legal parent*, a number of scenarios have to be kept distinct:

– where the artificial insemination procedure is performed on a *married woman*, her husband will be the child's legal father by virtue of the marital presumption in § 1592 No. 1 BGB. Where the *husband's sperm* is used, he obviously cannot contest his paternity pursuant to §§ 1600 *et seq.* BGB. Moreover, in a case of insemination by husband, even if the marriage has ended by the time of the child's birth (so that § 1592 No. 1 BGB no longer applies), the husband's paternity can be established by court order (§ 1592 No. 3 BGB) after the appropriate genetic tests.

If the *insemination was by donor*, on the other hand, the woman's husband will still be the child's legal father by virtue of § 1592 No. 1 BGB (provided that the parties are still married at the time of the child's birth). Although the husband is not the child's genetic parent in this case, since 2002, he has been barred from contesting his paternity by § 1600 IV BGB[91] *if* he has consented to the artificial insemination procedure in question. His consent does not have to be expressed in any particular form, although the 2006 *Musterrichtlinie* recommends that it be expressed in writing and signed.[92] The consent has to be given before the artificial insemination procedure in question[93] and can be revoked at any time and for any or no reason until conception has occurred.[94] Similarly, the mother is barred from contesting the husband's paternity if she has consented to the insemination procedure in question (§ 1600 IV BGB).

---

91   The provision was inserted (originally as § 1600 II BGB) by the *Gesetz zur weiteren Verbesserung von Kinderrechten* of April 9, 2002, BGBl. I, 1239.

92   (*Muster-*)*Richtlinie zur Durchführung der Assistierten Reproduktion* of February 17, 2006, para. 3.2.6.

93   MünchKomm/*Wellenhofer*, 7th ed. 2017, § 1600 para. 61.

94   BGH, NJW (2015): 3434.

A difficulty arises *if the marriage ends in divorce before the child is born*. In that case, the husband's paternity does not follow from the marital presumption in § 1592 No. 1 BGB, nor can it be established by court order pursuant to § 1592 No. 3 BGB because the husband is not the child's genetic parent. § 1600 IV BGB does not cover this situation either, since it removes only the right to *contest* an *existing* paternity. If the husband refuses to acknowledge paternity of the child pursuant to § 1592 No. 2 BGB, there is no way of forcing him to become the child's legal parent (at least absent a parentage contract[95]). The German Supreme Court has fashioned a partial way out of this unfortunate impasse. It interprets the husband's consent to the artificial insemination procedure as a contract to support the resulting child.[96] By these contractual means, at least some of the financial obligations of parenthood are imposed on the husband's shoulders, although it remains highly unsatisfactory that he should be able to renege on his promise to become the child's legal parent, with all of its attendant rights and responsibilities.

– Where the artificial insemination is performed on an *unmarried woman in a stable heterosexual relationship*, her male partner can become the child's legal father by *acknowledging paternity* of the child pursuant to § 1592 No. 2 BGB. He can acknowledge paternity before the child is born (§ 1594 IV BGB), but, at least according to the prevailing opinion in the case law and literature, he cannot do so before the child is conceived.[97] The reason customarily advanced for this rule is that an acknowledgment of paternity prior to conception would be made (implicitly) conditional on the child's being the outcome of a particular insemination procedure (rather than the mother's intercourse with a third party, for instance) and that an acknowledgment of paternity cannot be given conditionally, as is made clear by § 1594 III BGB. This argument seems highly formalistic and should not be allowed to conclude the matter. The interests of the parties to the insemination procedure—and, in particular, the interests of any child resulting from

---

95   For details on parentage contracts, see *infra* chap. 7.

96   BGH, NJW (2015): 3434.

97   MünchKomm/*Wellenhofer*, 7th ed. 2017, § 1594 para. 43; Stefan Wehrstedt, "Notarielle Vereinbarungen anlässlich einer künstlichen Befruchtung," RNotZ (2005): 109, 113. However, there are also those, including myself, who hold a different view, among them Jochen Taupitz and Julia Schlüter, "Heterologe künstliche Befruchtung: Die Absicherung des Samenspenders gegen unterhalts- und erbrechtliche Ansprüche des Kindes," AcP 205 (2005): 591, 595; Andreas Roth, "Der Ausschluss der Vaterschaftsanfechtung nach Einwilligung in die heterologe Insemination (§ 1600 Abs. 2 BGB)," DNotZ (2003): 805, 808 and Tobias Wilms, "Die künstliche Befruchtung in der notariellen Beratung," RNotZ (2012): 141, 145 et seq.

it—are best served by enhancing predictability and making sure that promises are kept. Hence, it should be possible to make binding commitments as to one's parental status before a child is on the way.[98]

If the male partner acknowledges paternity of the child, he cannot subsequently contest his paternity on the ground that he is not the child's genetic parent if he has consented to the donor insemination in question (§ 1600 IV BGB). If the male partner does not acknowledge paternity of the donor-conceived[99] child, on the other hand, then, as the law now stands, there is no way of forcing him to become the child's legal parent. As with a reneging husband, however, the male partner's consent to the artificial insemination procedure will be construed as a contract to support the child.[100]

A further potential problem arises if the child's mother does not consent to the acknowledgment of paternity (as she must for the acknowledgment to be valid (§ 1595 I BGB)). The prevailing view is that the mother's consent, like the acknowledgment of paternity itself, can be given prior to birth (§§ 1595 III, 1594 IV BGB), but that it cannot be given prior to conception. If the mother reneges, the man's route to legal paternity is closed off if donor sperm was used.

Can the *sperm donor* establish his paternity by a court order pursuant to § 1592 No. 3 BGB? What is clear is that as long as the paternity of another man exists—either that of the mother's husband pursuant to § 1592 No. 1 BGB or that of her male partner pursuant to § 1592 No. 2 BGB—the sperm donor's right to have his paternity established by court order is barred (§ 1600d I BGB). Moreover, the German Supreme Court has held that the sperm donor cannot remove this bar by contesting the paternity of the mother's husband or male partner, pursuant to § 1600 I No. 2 BGB. The sperm donor's right to contest the legal father's paternity is not expressly excluded by § 1600 IV BGB, which mentions only the right to contest of the woman and the man who consented to the donor insemination, intending to become the legal father of the resulting child. However, in 2013, the Supreme Court held that the legislature clearly intended to exclude the donor's right to contest the legal father's paternity in the scenario envisaged by § 1600 IV BGB— namely, in cases of insemination by donor of a woman living in a stable (married or unmarried) heterosexual relationship.[101]

---

98   For a more detailed discussion, see *infra* chap. 7 on parentage contracts.
99   If the male partner's sperm was used, on the other hand, his paternity can be established by court order pursuant to § 1592 No. 3 BGB (after the appropriate genetic tests).
100   BGH, NJW (2015): 3434.
101   BGH, NJW (2013): 2589, 2590.

– Where the insemination is performed on a *woman living in a lesbian marriage or in a lesbian registered partnership*, the mother's lesbian (marital or registered) partner does not come within the marital presumption of § 1592 No. 1 BGB and cannot acknowledge her co-maternity pursuant to § 1592 No. 2 BGB,[102] despite a minority view to the contrary.[103] This is because of the clear wording of § 1592 BGB, which bears the title "paternity" and opens with the words "the father of a child is the man, who....". As the law currently stands, the co-mother's parental status can be established only by adoption. As a married or registered partner, she can adopt her partner's child by way of a stepparent adoption, thus becoming the second legal parent of the child pursuant to §§ 1741 II 3, 1754 I BGB (for registered partners: § 9 VII LPartG). This possibility does not exist if the two women are neither spouses nor registered partners, but mere cohabitants. In that case, the possibility of a stepparent adoption does not exist, and the co-mother's adoption would necessarily terminate the birth mother's parental status (§ 1754 I, II BGB). This is almost never the desired result, however.

Problems can arise if either woman experiences a change of heart between the decision to undergo donor insemination and the making of the adoption order. An adoption order is made conditional on the consent of the child's birth parent(s) (in our case the birth mother and, possibly, the sperm donor[104]), the consent of the child,[105] and the consent of the adoptive parent(s) (§§ 1746, 1747 BGB). Because of § 1747 II 1 BGB, the *birth mother* can give binding consent only eight weeks after the child's birth. If she changes her mind about the adoption before that time, her partner will not usually[106] be able to acquire co-parental status. The mandatory eight-week delay in § 1747 II 1 BGB is intended to protect the birth mother from having to take the momentous decision to give up her child at a time of emotional turmoil during her pregnancy or immediately after giving birth. It may be

---

102   For the majority view, see, in particular, Christopher Schmidt, "Anwendung von § 1592 Nr. 1 auf Co-Mütter?," NZFam (2017): 832, 833.

103   For the minority view, see, in particular, Sabrina Binder and Arndt Kiehnle, "'Ehe für alle'—und Frauen als Männer," NZFam (2017): 742 et seq.; Martin Löhnig, "Ehe für alle—Abstammung für alle?," NZFam (2017): 643 et seq.; Mathias Zschiebsch, "Welche Auswirkungen hat das Gesetz 'Ehe für alle' auf das Adoptionsrecht?," notar (2017): 363.

104   On the necessity of the donor's consent, see the next paragraph below.

105   Note that in the case of a child under 14 years, the consent in question will be given by the child's legal representative, which, in our case, will normally be the birth mother (§ 1746 I 2 BGB).

106   The birth parent's consent can be dispensed with, according to § 1748 BGB, but the (extremely restrictive) conditions for doing so will almost never be present in an assisted reproduction scenario.

doubted, however, whether this protection is also necessary in stepparent adoptions complementing an assisted reproduction procedure. Unlike the typical mother who 'gives up' her child for adoption, the lesbian birth mother does not lose her own co-maternity. Her partner's stepparent adoption merely adds a second legal parent. What is more, the birth mother's pregnancy was planned with a view to a later stepparent adoption by her lesbian partner. This means that she had a chance to think about the adoption and its implications *prior to conception*, at a time when she was still free from the pressures and burdens of an existing pregnancy. As long as § 1747 II 1 BGB is not deleted or changed by the legislature, however, the co-mother's hopes of acquiring parental status may be thwarted by the birth mother's change of mind after the child is born, whatever her previous assurances to the contrary. In a similar fashion, the *adopting co-mother* can upset the couple's preconception plans by withdrawing her adoption application at any time before the order is made.[107]

The *sperm donor*, on the other hand, is unlikely to constitute an obstacle. His consent to the adoption (if one requires it at all, about which more momentarily) can be given prior to birth (§ 1747 III No. 1 BGB). What is more: it would appear that the donor can consent to the adoption prior to conception. This is because the argument (formalistic and unconvincing as it is, to my mind) that is urged by the majority against allowing acknowledgments of paternity prior to conception–namely, that such acknowledgments are subject to an impermissible[108] (implied) condition—does not apply to the sperm donor. The sperm donor's consent to the adoption is not subject to an implied condition. Rather, the donor consents unconditionally to the adoption of any child of the birth mother. If the child turns out not to have been conceived with his sperm, his consent is simply irrelevant. The only potential problem with the donor's preconception consent arises from the fact that any consent to an adoption becomes binding only when it is filed with the family court. However, there is no reason why the donor should not be able to file at the earliest opportunity: before the adoption application or even before the insemination procedure. The law does not prescribe any particular chronological order for the various declarations that have to be

---

107 OLG Düsseldorf, FamRZ (1997): 117; BeckOK/*Pöcker*, BGB, 45th ed., § 1752 para. 3.
108 According to § 1750 II 1 BGB, an acknowledgment of paternity has to be given unconditionally.

made before an adoption decree can be issued; it only requires that all of these declarations be present at the time of the adoption decree.[109]

The donor's consent to the adoption may not even be required at all. According to a 2015 decision by the German Supreme Court, the sperm donor is excluded from participation in the adoption proceedings if he has, from the very start, waived "his constitutionally protected interest to become the legal father of the child."[110] This waiver requires no particular form, but it could be expressed in a notarial or signed document, for instance.

– Where the donor insemination is carried out on a *single woman* without a permanent male or lesbian partner, the intention of the parties to the procedure usually is for the child to have just one legal parent: the birth mother. This is a result that the medical profession, by denying access to medically assisted artificial reproductive procedures to single women through its 2006 *Musterrichtlinie*,[111] is, or at least was, actively trying to avoid. However, in practice, insemination procedures are performed on or by single women, without—and sometimes even with—medical assistance. If neither the woman nor the sperm donor nor the child takes any steps towards establishing the sperm donor's paternity, the child will grow up with just one legal parent—a result that, as I argued above, is acceptable and no cause for grave concern.

But what happens if one of the parties principally concerned (that is, the woman, the sperm donor, or the child) wants to establish the *sperm donor's paternity*? The answer to that question has changed as of July 1, 2018:

Prior to that date, it was clear that the child could apply for a court order establishing the sperm donor's paternity, pursuant to § 1592 No. 3 BGB. So could the woman and the sperm donor—at least in the absence of a parentage contract waiving this right (on which more below).[112]

As a result of the *Gesetz zur Regelung der Kenntnis der Abstammung bei heterologer Verwendung von Samen*[113] of July 17, 2017,[114] the new § 1600d IV BGB was inserted with effect from July 1, 2018. According to the new provision, the sperm donor's paternity can no longer be established if the child in question was created through a medically assisted artificial reproductive procedure

---

109   On the permissibility of consenting to an adoption prior to the filing of an adoption application, see BayObLG, FamRZ (1983): 761 and MünchKomm/*Maurer*, 7th ed. 2017, § 1750 para. 37.

110   BGH, NJW (2015): 1820, 1822.

111   (*Muster-*)*Richtlinie zur Durchführung der Assistierten Reproduktion* of February 17, 2006, para 3.1.1.

112   See *infra* chap. 7.

113   In English: Act on the Right to Know One's Genetic Origins in Donor Insemination Cases.

114   BGBl. I, 2513.

in a medical facility within the meaning of § 1a No. 9 *Transplantationsgesetz* (Transplantation Act) with the use of donor sperm that was provided to a sperm bank within the meaning of § 2 I 1 *Samenspenderregistergesetz* (Sperm Donors' Registration Act). It does not matter who—whether it be the mother, the sperm donor, or the child—brings the application. Where the restrictive conditions of § 1600d IV BGB are not met, however— that is, where either the sperm was not officially donated or the insemi- nation was carried out without medical assistance—the law continues as before. In that case, the right to have the sperm donor's paternity estab- lished is not excluded as a matter of law. (On the possibility of excluding this right by means of a parentage contract, see chapter 7.)

5   *The Right to Know One's Genetic Origins and Children of Assisted Reproduction*

In light of the positive experiences with adopted children (on these, see Part 1, paragraph 2.4), the recommendation is for children of assisted reproduction with donor sperm to be informed of their genetic origins at an early opportu- nity as well. Generally, young children display a neutral or interested reaction to the information that they were born with the help of sperm donation. And older children, who have grown up in the knowledge that they owe their exis- tence to a sperm donor, usually report that they can accept the fact and that the information does not negatively influence their relationship with their legal parents.[115]

The German Supreme Court has stressed that the child's right to know his or her genetic origins is constitutionally protected[116] and may be of funda- mental importance to the development of the child's personal identity.[117] A child born of assisted reproduction therefore has a *right to know the identity of the sperm donor*, although this right is not absolute. The right exists as *against the child's legal parents*, but also as *against the fertility clinic* at which the assist- ed reproductive procedure was performed. This is important, since the clinic is usually more likely to have the relevant information. The Supreme Court interprets the medical treatment contract between the fertility clinic and the child's parents as a contract with protective effect for the child.[118] This contrac- tual relationship in conjunction with the duty of good faith (§ 242 BGB) gives

---

115   Kindler et al., "Kenntnis der Abstammung bei fragmentierter Elternschaft aus humanwis- senschaftlicher Sicht," 932.

116   BVerfG 1989, 891 (right to know one's genetic origins protected by Arts 2 I, 1 GG).

117   BGH, NJW (2015): 1098, 1102.

118   BGH, NJW (2015): 1098, 1099.

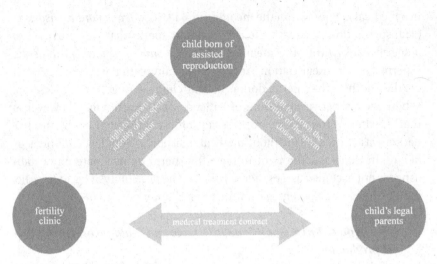

FIGURE 6   Illustration by author

the child a right, as against the clinic, to be informed about the identity of the sperm donor.

The right is not tied to the child's having reached a certain minimum age. As the Supreme Court points out, a child's interest in his or her genetic origins exists from the moment of birth and does not suddenly spring into being when the child turns sixteen or some other age. It is up to the parents to decide when and how they inform their minor children about the circumstances of their birth and the fact that they were born with the help of sperm donation. This decision-making power in the parents would be prejudiced, however, if the right to information about the sperm donor were tied to an age requirement.[119]

The right to information is *not absolute*. It exists only if the demand is *just and reasonable* having regard to the interests of other parties. Whether this test is met has to be determined in an individualized assessment that takes account of the (constitutional) rights and interests involved on both sides.[120] The Supreme Court has stressed, however, that the child's right carries a heavy weight and that it will usually override both the clinic's constitutional right to pursue a trade or profession (art. 12 Grundgesetz (GG)) and the sperm donor's constitutional right to informational self-determination (which forms an integral part of the personality right protected by Arts. 2 I, 1 GG).[121] This is correct, since the man who decides to become an official sperm donor makes a

119   BGH, NJW (2015): 1098, 1100.
120   BGH, NJW (2015): 1098, 1101.
121   BGH, NJW (2015): 1098, 1103 *et seq.*

conscious decision and is in a position to weigh up the potential consequences ahead of time.

The informational rights of children born of medically assisted reproduction were recently given an additional boost. In 2017, the German legislature adopted the *Gesetz zur Errichtung eines Samenspenderregisters und zur Regelung der Auskunftserteilung über den Spender nach heterologer Verwendung von Samen* (or *Samenspenderregistergesetz* ('SaRegG')).[122] The Act establishes a register of sperm donors to be kept by the German Institute for Medical Documentation and Information. The purpose of the register is to safeguard the right to know one's genetic origins for persons born of medically assisted artificial insemination procedures using donor sperm (§ 1 SaRegG).

When collecting sperm for an assisted insemination procedure, the sperm-collecting facility has to obtain and store the following information from the donor (§ 2 II SaRegG):

1.   family name and birth name (if different);
2.   first name;
3.   date and place of birth
4.   nationality
5.   address.

With the donor's written consent, the sperm-collecting facility also has to store the donor's additional statements about himself and about his motives for the donation. The donor's consent to the storage of this additional information may be withdrawn at any time (§ 2 III SaRegG). In the event of a withdrawal, the additional information stored pursuant to § 2 III SaRegG has to be deleted forthwith (§ 2 IV 4 SaRegG).

According to § 5 I 1, II SaRegG, a medical facility may use donor sperm for medically assisted artificial insemination only if it collects and stores the exact code allowing identification of the donor; the family name (and if different, the birth name), first name, date and place of birth and address of the woman receiving the sperm; and the name and address of the sperm-collecting facility. Once the medical facility learns of the birth of the child (most likely from the child's mother, who is under a duty to report the birth within three months of its taking place pursuant to § 4 sent. 3 SaRegG), it has to pass on its stored information to the German Institute for Medical Documentation and Information (§ 6 I SaRegG). The Institute may require the sperm-collecting facility to pass on the information that is stored there (§ 6 IV SaRegG). The Institute has to store all the information reported to or gathered by it for a period of 110 years

---

122   BGBl. I, 2513. In English, the title would read: 'Act to Establish a Register for Sperm Donors and to Regulate Access to Information about the Donor after Insemination with Donor Sperm.'

(§ 8 sent. 1 SaRegG). Any person who suspects that he or she may have been born as a result of a medically assisted reproductive procedure using donor sperm has a right to information as against the German Institute for Medical Documentation and Information. The right consists in obtaining the personal data of the donor whose sperm was used for the insemination of the applicant's mother (§ 10 I SaRegG). If voluntary statements by the donor are stored in accordance with § 2 III 1 SaRegG, they are covered by the duty of disclosure as well (§ 10 II SaRegG).

While much has been done, therefore, to safeguard the informational rights of children born of *medically assisted* reproductive procedures, the rights of children born of private insemination procedures are still quite unprotected. These children do not benefit from the informational rights granted by the *Samenspenderregistergesetz* nor do they have a right to information as against a medical treatment facility since no medical facility was involved in their creation. In theory, they have a right to information as against their mother. However, this right may come to nothing if the child does not know that he or she was born with the help of sperm donation (which may happen if the parents decide to keep the donation a secret, for instance) or if the mother does not know the donor's identity.

6   *The Position of Sperm Donors*

There are *two ways to donate sperm*, which have to be kept distinct: first, sperm may be donated *officially to a sperm-collecting facility* within the meaning of § 2 I SaRegG, for use in a medically assisted artificial reproduction procedure. Sperm donors who choose the official route do not normally know or come into contact with the intending parents, although there are exceptions: for instance, the intending parents may recruit a friend to make a sperm donation at an official sperm-collecting facility, but for the exclusive use of the intending parents (exclusive donor). Secondly, sperm may be donated *privately*—that is, outside of an official collecting facility. Colloquially, this is known as a *'Becherspende'* (in English, 'sperm in a cup'). Although it is more likely that there will be some degree of familiarity between the donor and the intending parents in a private donation scenario, this is not necessarily the case. Judging from reported cases, many intending parents 'meet' their donor online and sometimes never learn his true identity.[123]

---

123   For two recent private donation cases in which the intending parents did not know the donor's identity, see BGH, NJW (2015): 1820; OLG Bamberg, FamRZ (2017): 1236.

There are many reasons why men may choose to become sperm donors. A financial motive is usually not one of them, however, at least in official donations. As the term 'donation' implies, donors are not remunerated for their services, although they are compensated for their time and out-of-pocket expenses. Normally, German sperm banks pay a flat rate of between 80 and 130 euros for every usable donation of sperm.[124] Some donors are open to the idea of contact ('yes donors'[125]). However, sperm donors do not normally intend to become the social—let alone the legal—parents of the children who are conceived with their sperm.

In view of the usual intention *not* to become the legal father of the child, until relatively recently, a *sperm donor* was engaged in a fairly risky business, for he *could have his paternity established against his will*. This could happen where the intending parents' marriage had ended by the time of the birth; where the parents were never married to begin with; or where the donation was for a lesbian couple or a single woman. In all these cases, unless a voluntary acknowledgment of paternity by the ex-husband or male partner or an adoption by the lesbian co-mother intervened, there was no legal bar to the establishment of the sperm donor's paternity by court order pursuant to §§ 1592 No. 3, 1600d I BGB. While it was unclear whether the intending parents could contract away their right to have the sperm donor's paternity established,[126] it was clear that they could not contract away *the child's*. As a result, sperm donors ran the risk of incurring hefty support obligations and of rendering their estates subject to forced share claims by their donor children.

For some sperm donors, this risk has been removed as of July 1, 2018. As a result of the *new § 1600d IV BGB*,[127] a sperm donor's paternity can no longer be established (on anyone's application), if the sperm was donated to an official collecting facility within the meaning of § 2 I SaRegG for use in a medically assisted artificial reproductive procedure. For private donors, on the other hand, the risk continues unabated. One way to guard against (some of) the financial aspects of that risk is to sign a parentage contract, in which the intending parents agree to indemnify the donor for any support payments or other

---

124 Cryobank München pays 80 euros per donation (https://www.cryobank-muenchen.de/Samenspende/Verguetung, last accessed July 9, 2018) whereas Erlanger Samenbank pays 130 euros (https://www.erlanger-samenbank.de/, last accessed July 9, 2018).

125 For the differentiation into 'yes' and 'no' donors, see Arbeitskreis Abstammungsrecht, *Abschlussbericht*, 54 et seq.

126 For the view against, see MünchKomm/*Wellenhofer*, 7th ed. 2017, § 1600, para. 72.

127 Inserted by *Gesetz zur Regelung des Rechts auf Kenntnis der Abstammung bei heterologer Verwendung von Samen* of July 17, 2017 (BGBl. I, 2513).

Official Donation	Private Donation
• regulated by § 2 I SaRegG • sperm donated **officially to a sperm-collecting facility** • for use in a medically assisted artificial reproduction procedure • → **§ 1600d IV BGB:** donor's paternity can no longer be established on anyone's application	• no legal framework • → donor's paternity can be established on child's application

FIGURE 7   Illustration by author

expenses incurred by him after being established as the child's father on the child's application.

Despite the donor's usual intention not to become the legal father of the child, there have also been cases in which *the donor himself tried to have his paternity established* against the wishes of the intending parent(s). In the case of a preexisting paternity in the intending father pursuant to § 1592 Nos. 1 or 2 BGB, the sperm donor's claim is barred (see § 1600 I BGB). And since the Supreme Court has opted for an expansive interpretation of § 1600 IV BGB (by holding that the donor's right to contest the intending father's paternity is also implicitly excluded by that provision),[128] the donor cannot remove that bar by contesting the preexisting paternity. Where the position of legal father is not yet occupied, on the other hand (in particular in sperm donations for lesbian couples), then, according to one opinion, the donor can withhold his consent to the stepparent adoption and pursue his paternity claim, whatever his prior assurances to the contrary.[129] This view seems hard to maintain, however, in light of a decision by the Supreme Court in 2015. In it, the Supreme Court indicated that a sperm donor can, even at the time of his donation, "waive his constitutionally protected right to become the legal father of the child"[130] and that he can do so even outside the scenario covered by § 1600 IV BGB (the case before the Court concerned a private sperm donation for lesbian registered partners). The Court went on to state that a waiver can usually be assumed in the case of an anonymous donation.[131] According to the Supreme Court,

---

128   BGH, NJW (2013): 2589, 2590.
129   MünchKomm/*Wellenhofer*, 7th ed. 2017, § 1600 para. 74.
130   BGH, NJW (2015): 1820, 1822.
131   BGH, NJW (2015): 1820, 1821.

where the donor has waived his rights, he does not even have to be notified of the adoption proceedings, let alone consent to the adoption.[132]

7 Parentage Contracts

Because the German legislature has so far failed to enact comprehensive legislation dealing with the complex legal issues arising from artificial reproduction, many areas of uncertainty remain. This has given rise to the question whether the existing gaps can be filled in by private contracting. In other words: can the parties to an artificial reproductive procedure enter into a binding contractual agreement about the allocation of parental status for the resulting child?

In answering that question, it is best to keep the following scenarios distinct:

(1) **Donor Insemination for a Heterosexual Married Couple**

This is the scenario best catered for by the legislature. The intending father's paternity follows from the marital presumption in § 1592 No. 1 BGB. In 2002, the legislature inserted § 1600 II BGB (now § 1600 IV BGB),[133] which prevents the intending parents from contesting the man's paternity if they have consented to the insemination procedure in question. The Supreme Court, as we have seen, basing itself on the implied intent of the legislature, has interpreted the provision expansively, to exclude the right of contest of the sperm donor as well.[134] As a result, there is little need for private contracting where donor insemination is performed on a married couple. Of course, the 'consent' required by § 1600 IV BGB itself imports a contractual element.

(2) **Donor Insemination for a Heterosexual Unmarried Couple**

In this case, the intending father's paternity does not follow from the marital presumption, but requires an acknowledgment of paternity pursuant to § 1592 No. 2 BGB. This, in its turn, requires the consent of the intending father and that of the mother (§ 1595 I BGB). As previously mentioned, according to the majority view, although the man's acknowledgment and the woman's consent thereto can be given before the child is born (§§ 1594 IV, 1595 III), neither declaration can be given before the child is *conceived*.[135] The majority argues that any such declaration would be tied to the implied condition that the child is the result of a particular assisted reproductive procedure (and not of the mother's intercourse with a third

---

132 BGH, NJW (2015): 1820, 1821. For a similar ruling by a lower court, see OLG Bamberg, FamRZ (2017): 1236.

133 *Gesetz zur weiteren Verbesserung von Kinderrechten* of April 9, 2002, BGBl. I, 1239.

134 BGH, NJW (2013): 2589, 2590.

135 MünchKomm/*Wellenhofer*, 7th ed. 2017, § 1594, para. 43; *Wehrstedt*, "Notarielle Vereinbarungen anlässlich einer künstlichen Befruchtung," 113.

party, for instance) and that § 1594 III BGB and § 1595 III BGB require that the acknowledgment and the consent be given unconditionally.

This argument, as previously stated, seems highly formalistic. However, even if one accepts it, there would seem to be no reason why the parties should not be able to enter into a contractual agreement *prior to conception*, binding themselves to make the required declarations *after* the child has been conceived. The contractual obligation in question would, of course, relate only to a child conceived of a particular reproductive procedure, and the man would not be in breach of contract if he refused to acknowledge a child conceived at some other time or by some other means (which could be established by genetic testing, where appropriate).[136] Contractual rights and duties can certainly be made conditional, and the condition in question is perfectly legitimate. Still, for many, the idea of a preconceptual contract to acknowledge a child is unpalatable, and even disturbing. This probably stems from an understandable desire to keep intimate interactions free from the strictures of contract.[137] Preconceptual parentage contracts to acknowledge a child are still little used in practice, and their enforceability remains uncertain.[138]

(3) **Donor Insemination for a Lesbian Registered or Married Couple**

As we have seen, as the law stands, parental status for the lesbian married or registered partner requires a stepparent adoption and cannot be brought about by a simple acknowledgment of co-maternity. According to § 1747 II 1 BGB, moreover, the birth mother can consent to the stepparent adoption only eight weeks after the child's birth. This clear provision rules out binding contractual agreements to consent to the adoption before the eight-week period has elapsed. Similarly, the mother's partner cannot contractually bind herself to file the adoption application,[139] and, even after an application has been filed, a right of revocation exists until the adoption order is made (§ 1750 IV 1 BGB).[140] The sperm donor, on the other hand, can consent to the adoption preconceptually. His consent,

---

136 For this argument, see, e.g., Taupitz and Schlüter, "Heterologe künstliche Befruchtung," 596.

137 The German Supreme Court has held, e.g., that contracts about the use of contraceptive devices between intimate partners are unenforceable (BGH, NJW (1986): 2043).

138 Grziwotz is doubtful as to their enforceability: see Herbert Grziwotz, "Künstliche Fortpflanzung und Vertragsgestaltung (Kinderwunschverträge)," in *Künstliche Fortpflanzung und europäisches Familienrecht*, ed. Anatol Dutta et al. (Bielefeld: Gieseking, 2015), 34 et seq.

139 Grziwotz, "Künstliche Fortpflanzung und Vertragsgestaltung," 51 et seq.

140 OLG Düsseldorf, FamRZ (1997): 117; BeckOK/*Pöcker*, 45th ed., § 1752, para. 3.

even where it is given prior to conception, is not tied to an (impermissible (see § 1750 II 1 BGB)) condition: if the child turns out not to have been conceived with his sperm, his consent to the child's adoption is simply irrelevant. What is more, according to a 2015 decision by the Supreme Court, the sperm donor does not even have to be notified of the adoption proceedings, let alone give his consent to the adoption, if he has waived his "constitutionally protected interest to become the legal father of the child."[141] Such a waiver could certainly form part of a parentage contract.

To sum up: the third scenario does not lend itself very well to parentage contracts since the intending co-mothers cannot enter into a binding agreement until fairly late. Therefore, the sperm donor is at risk of having his paternity established (and of being exposed to support obligations and forced share claims) should the intending mothers change their mind about the adoption later on. Again, a parentage contract can help to an extent, by providing for a right of indemnity against the intending mothers.

(4) Donor Insemination for a Single Woman

Where the donor insemination is performed on a single woman, the intention of the parties is usually the same as that of the parties in the other three scenarios: to avoid legal paternity in the sperm donor. We have seen that, in the other three scenarios, this intention can be given effect by means of a parentage contract. The parties can waive their right to contest the intending father's paternity (to the extent that this right is not already excluded by law because of § 1600 IV BGB) and they can waive their right to participate in adoption proceedings. Can the same result be achieved where the donor insemination is performed on a single woman? The difference to the other three scenarios consists in the fact that, in this case, the parentage contract does not seek to replace a genetic with an intending parent (leaving the child with two legal parents). It aims to leave the child with just one legal parent: the birth mother.

Where the insemination meets the conditions of § 1600d IV BGB (that is, where the child is created from officially donated sperm in a medically assisted procedure), the right to have the donor's paternity established is excluded for all parties involved. However, this result is brought about by operation of law. It is not brought about by a parentage contract. The question is whether the right to have the donor's paternity established can be excluded by a parentage contract in cases not covered by § 1600d IV BGB. This issue is controversial, but in my opinion the answer has to be in the affirmative.

---

141   BGH, NJW (2015): 1820, 1822.

As the German Constitutional Court has pointed out, it is not having fewer, but having *more* than two parents that can lead to difficulties because of conflicting roles and disputes about areas of authority.[142] Single parenthood does not pose these risks, nor are there any other legitimate objections to it, as is implicitly recognized by the fact that single persons may adopt (§ 1741 II 1 BGB). In our fourth scenario, the effect of the parentage contract is similar to a lawful single-parent adoption. The only difference is that there is no child welfare assessment. However, this seems justified by the fact that, in our scenario, the child's single parent is not a stranger, but the child's genetic mother. While it is true that any child should have two legal parents, wherever possible,[143] it is important to bear in mind that the child's rights are not compromised by the parentage contract between the donor and the mother. A parentage contract between the donor and the mother can only waive the contracting parties' right to have the donor's paternity established; it cannot waive or take away the *child's*. A refusal to treat the donor's and the mother's waiver of rights as binding, on the other hand, would enable the donor to force his way into the life of mother and child against his previous assertions, or to make the mother pay for him to abstain from doing so. The mother's only hope of relief from this unpleasant situation would be to find a third party willing to acknowledge paternity, thus generally blocking the donor's road to establishing his own paternity (§§ 1600d I BGB, 1600 I No. 2, II BGB). In the case of a single woman, a suitable third party may not be available, however, or available only at a price.

8   *Procreative Tourism and Its Implications for Domestic German Courts*

The treatment standards on assisted reproduction in Germany have to be seen in a European—and even an international—context. They are not unaffected by technological advances and—perhaps less restrictive—legal and ethical standards elsewhere. There are significant national differences in the allocation of parental status for children of assisted reproduction. This is particularly true for national definitions of motherhood, with an increasing number of countries, even European ones such as Greece, Great Britain, and the Netherlands,[144] allowing surrogacy, for instance, and granting parental status to the woman

---

142   BVerfG, NJW (2003): 2151, 2153.

143   Martin Löhnig, "Zivilrechtliche Aspekte der Samenspende de lege ferenda," ZRP (2015): 76.

144   Eleni Zervogianni, "Künstliche Fortpflanzung im griechischen Recht," in *Künstliche Fortpflanzung und europäisches Familienrecht*, ed. Anatol Dutta et al. (Bielefeld: Gieseking, 2015), 216 et seq.; Claudia Campbell, "Das Verbot der Leihmutterschaft," NJW-Spezial (2018): 196.

who intends to become the legal mother of the child. Other countries allocate parental status to same-sex parents without the need for an adoption order, which is still required by German law. As a result, the allocation of parental status for children of assisted reproduction may well differ according to the applicable national law. It follows that the rules of private international law, which determine which legal system governs and which national law applies, acquire particular importance.

1 Determining the Applicable Law

The German private international law rules on descent and parentage are mainly[145] contained in *art 19 Einführungsgesetz zum Bürgerlichen Gesetzbuch* (Introductory Act to the Civil Code, 'EGBGB'), which applies to marital and non-marital children and to the determination of paternal as well as maternal status alike. Somewhat unusually, it provides for *several connecting factors* of equal rank. According to art. 19 I 1 EGBGB, parental status for a child is governed by the law of the state of the child's habitual residence. Alternatively, parental status for the child can be determined, but only in relation to each potential parent, according to the law of the state of that parent's citizenship (art. 19 I 2 EGBGB). Finally, where the child's mother is married, parentage may be determined according to the law governing the general effects of her marriage (with that law being determined in accordance with art. 14 EGBGB).

The different connecting factors are *of equal rank*.[146] Where the connecting factors point to different legal systems, precedence is given to the law that is *best for the child*.[147] Sometimes that determination is easy. Take the following example: a German woman and her Swedish non-marital male partner, both resident in Germany, undergo an artificial insemination procedure using donor sperm. After the child is born, the couple separate and the Swedish intending father does not acknowledge paternity. If one determines the applicable law in accordance with art. 19 I 1 EGBGB, German law applies, since the child's habitual residence is in Germany. According to German law, establishing a parent–child relationship between a child and a man who is not married to the child's mother and not genetically the child's father requires an acknowledgment of paternity (§ 1592 No. 2 BGB). If German law were to govern, therefore, the child would be fatherless. In contrast, art. 19 I 2 EGBGB points to Swedish

---

145 There are special conflicts rules for contesting parentage (art. 20 EGBGB) and for consenting to an acknowledgment of paternity or maternity (art. 23 EGBGB).

146 BGH, FamRZ (2016): 1251, 1253; 2016, 1847, 1848; MünchKomm/*Helms*, 7th ed. 2018, art. 19 EGBGB para. 12.

147 KG, FamRZ (2015): 922, 923; OLG Hamm, FamRZ (2009): 126, 128.

law as the law of the man's country of citizenship for establishing his parental status. Under Swedish law, the woman's non-marital partner is treated as the child's legal father if he consented to the donor insemination.[148] In this case, it is pretty obvious that the better law for the child is Swedish law.

Sometimes, however, all available connecting factors lead to unpalatable results. To illustrate: a German couple enters into a surrogacy agreement in Georgia. In accordance with Georgian law, their names are entered as the child's legal parents on the child's birth certificate. When the parents try to bring the child to Germany, however, they are refused entry. In this case, the connecting factors in art. 19 I 2 EGBGB leave the child with no legal mother. German law (§ 1591 BGB) categorically denies parental status to the German intending mother. However, Georgian law—the law of the surrogate's country of citizenship and hence the law applicable to determining her parental status under art. 19 I 2 EGBGB—refuses to treat the surrogate as the legal mother if the intending mother's name is entered on the birth certificate.[149] Article 19 I 1 EGBGB does not yield a preferable result, either. The habitual residence of children usually follows that of the persons taking care of them. Because the German couple intends to take the child to Germany at the earliest opportunity, the child's habitual residence will be Germany, even if the child is physically present in Georgia for the time being.[150] German law, however, refuses to treat the intending mother as the child's legal mother. Paradoxically, the situation may improve *after* the child has been refused entry.[151] From that moment, the child's physical presence in Georgia is likely to be of sufficient duration to qualify as a habitual residence, leading to the application of Georgian law pursuant to art. 19 I 1 EGBGB. Georgian law, however, assigns legal parenthood to the German couple. If this result is recognized by the German authorities (which depends on whether there is a conflict with public policy (also known as the German *ordre public*, on which more below)), the German couple acquire the status of the child's legal parents and will be allowed to take it back to Germany.

---

148 Tobias Helms, "Künstliche Fortpflanzung und Internationales Privatrecht," in *Künstliche Fortpflanzung und europäisches Familienrecht*, ed. Anatol Dutta et al. (Bielefeld: Gieseking, 2015), 62.

149 Irma Gelashvili, "Legal and Ethical Problems of Surrogacy," *Tbilisi State University Journal of Law* (2011): 77 et seq.

150 OLG Celle, FamRZ (2011): 1518, 1519.

151 Bettina Heiderhoff, "Rechtliche Abstammung im Ausland geborener Leihmutterkinder," NJW (2014): 2673, 2675.

2   Recognition of Foreign Parentage Determinations by German Courts

The applicable law is irrelevant if a foreign court has already ruled on the parental status of the child.[152] Decisions by foreign courts and certain other foreign authorities are recognized pursuant to §§ 108, 109 FamFG (the German Code of Procedure in Family Matters). These generous provisions apply only to determinations by foreign courts and foreign authorities; they do not apply to entries in foreign civil registers. § 109 FamFG contains a list of grounds for refusing recognition, the most important of which is § 109 I No. 4 FamFG, which precludes recognition if recognizing the foreign decision would lead to results that are in obvious conflict with the German *ordre public*.

3   The *Ordre Public* Exception

The *ordre public* exception comes into play where art. 19 EGBGB leads to the application of foreign law (art. 6 EGBGB). It is also relevant to the recognition of foreign determinations of parentage (§ 109 I No. 4 FamFG). The purpose of the exception is to prevent the application of foreign law or the recognition of a foreign decision where the application or recognition in question would present an intolerable conflict with the basic values of Germany's legal order. Whether such a conflict exists is not determined in the abstract, however, but with reference to the actual result that the application or recognition would have in a particular case.

The *ordre public* exception is most frequently discussed with reference to surrogacy arrangements entered into by German couples, but carried out abroad. Where the arrangement in question is governed by a surrogacy-friendly foreign law or where a foreign court has recognized the parental status of the intending parents, the question becomes whether accepting this result would be in conflict with the German policy against surrogacy.

The *ECtHR* has laid down the fundamental principles in two leading decisions of 2014 and 2017.[153] The first case involved the refusal of French authorities to recognize a Californian judgment allocating parental status to a French couple who had entered into a surrogacy arrangement in California. The children were the genetic offspring of the husband. The Court recognized that assisted reproduction is a sensitive and controversial area, involving complicated questions of ethics and morals, about which there is no European consensus. Hence, member states have a wide margin of appreciation. The Court found no violation of the couple's right to family life guaranteed by ECHR, art. 8, since

152   Campbell, "Das Verbot der Leihmutterschaft," 196.
153   ECtHR, NJW (2015): 3211 (Mennesson, France); (2017), 941 (Paradiso and Campanelli, Italy).

the non-recognition of their parental status did not prevent them from living together as a family in France.[154] It did, however, find a breach of the children's right to respect for private life, which is also guaranteed by ECHR, art. 8. The Court reasoned that an essential aspect of the children's identity was involved, because the children could not be sure of acquiring French citizenship or of being recognized as the legal heirs of their French parents.[155] This contradiction between the legal and social realities undermined the children's identity within French society. Considering the consequences for the identity of the children and their right to respect for private life, the Court found that France had exceeded the wide margin of appreciation left to member states in the sphere of surrogacy.[156]

The second decision involved an Italian couple who had hired a surrogate in Moscow. The chief difference from the earlier case was that the child was not genetically related to either intending parent. Six months after the couple's return to Italy, the Italian authorities placed the baby, first, in a children's home and, two years later, with foster parents, denying all contact to the applicants. The Court found that, having regard to the absence of any biological tie between the child and the intending parents, the short duration of the relationship with the child, and the uncertainty of the ties from a legal perspective (itself a direct result of the couple's decision to circumvent the Italian ban on surrogacy), the conditions for a de facto family life had not been established. Hence, the right to respect for family life protected by ECHR, art. 8 was inapplicable.[157] The Court also found there to have been no breach of the right to respect for private life. While there was a burden on the applicants' private life (namely, their decision to become and act as parents), that burden was justified because it was proportionate to the legitimate aim of preventing a trade in children in contravention of French adoption law. Where the foreign surrogacy in question involves no genetic link between the child and the intending parents, the ECtHR would thus seem to have opened the door to considerations of public policy (namely, the need to deter illegal practices), provided that the child's welfare is not compromised.[158]

In applying the European Court's principles, the German courts have, in the main, treated the child's interest in maintaining established family ties as paramount. As a result, they have tended to accept foreign surrogacy arrangements

---

154   ECtHR, NJW (2015): 3211, 3216 (Mennesson, France).
155   ECtHR, NJW (2015): 3211, 3216 (Mennesson, France).
156   ECtHR, NJW (2015): 3211, 3217 (Mennesson, France).
157   ECtHR, NJW (2017): 941, 943 (Paradiso and Campanelli, Italy).
158   Martin Löhnig, "Die Leihmutterschaft in der aktuellen Rechtsprechung," NZFam (2017): 546, 548 is critical of the decision.

as a *fait accompli* and to abstain from invoking the public policy exception in art. 6 EGBGB and § 109 I No. 4 FamFG.[159] The Higher Regional Court of Braunschweig, however, recently—and somewhat surprisingly—arrived at a different conclusion in a case that involved both an egg donor and a surrogate, and where the intending father's paternity was uncertain.[160]

9   *Proposals for Reform*

The current legal framework for assisted reproduction in Germany is patchy and riddled with inconsistencies. Much is left to professional self-regulation; in many cases, the status consequences may not be known or settled before conception, which undermines legal certainty for the parties involved; the procedures for acquiring parentage discriminate between heterosexual and homosexual couples; and, while some forms of assisted reproduction remain outlawed in Germany, the courts generally have no choice but to accept the selfsame forms once they have resulted in the birth of a child.

In view of this unsatisfactory state of affairs, it is no surprise that there have been many calls for reform. In 2015, the then Minister of Justice, Heiko Maas, set up a working group (*Arbeitskreis Abstammungsrecht*) to make proposals for a new law of descent and parentage that would accommodate modern forms of reproduction. The working group's proposals[161] included:

- retaining the current definition of legal motherhood;
- opening co-parent status to men and women alike;
- making consent to a reproductive procedure the basis for allocating parental status in medically assisted donor insemination cases;
- strengthening the child's right to know his or her genetic origins.

Unfortunately, so far, nothing much has been done in terms of actual legislation. The current German government's coalition agreement envisages "changes to the law of descent and parentage, having due regard to the proposals submitted by the working group."[162] Whether this is more than lip service, however, remains to be seen.

---

159   OLG Celle, NZFam (2017): 658; KG, NJW (2017): 3241; OLG Düsseldorf, NJW (2015): 3382; BGH, DNotZ (2015): 296.

160   OLG Braunschweig, FuR (2017): 512.

161   The full text is available at www.bmjv.de.

162   Ein neuer Aufbruch für Europa, eine neue Dynamik für Deutschland, ein neuer Zusammenhalt für unser Land—Koalitionsvertrag zwischen CDU, CSU und SPD of March 12, 2018, 132.

Conclusion

Both the German law on adoption and the German law on assisted reproduction seem to be in need of reform. The current regulatory framework for adoption is more than four decades old, and no longer caters for the social reality of adoption, which has changed significantly from the 'old paradigm' of adoptions of young children by strangers to adult, in-family, and lesbian co-parent adoptions. As the law stands, the institution may be abused for collateral purposes (as in adult adoptions) or pressed into service to remedy the defects of other areas of the law (as in lesbian co-parent adoptions). A reform should both reorient the central institution and remove the incentive (or need) for the 'misuse' of adoption by reforming adjacent legal areas, and in particular the rules on filiation for lesbian couples who undergo donor insemination. When it comes to assisted reproduction, a comprehensive legislative response is long overdue. The sensitive legal issues raised by this fast-growing industry and social practice must not be left to professional self-regulation and piecemeal legislative tinkering any longer.

Bibliography

Arbeitskreis Abstammungsrecht. *Abschlussbericht*. Köln: Bundesanzeiger Verlag, 2017.

Beck'scher Online-Kommentar. 45th ed.

Bergschneider, Ludwig, ed. *Beck'sches Formularhandbuch Familienrecht*. 5th ed. Munich: Beck, 2017.

Binder, Sabrina, and Arndt Kiehnle. "'Ehe für alle'—und Frauen als Männer." *Neue Zeitschrift für Familienrecht* (2017): 742.

Bundesarbeitsgemeinschaft der Landesjugendämter. *Empfehlungen zur Adoptionsvermittlung*. 7th ed. 2014.

Bundesministerium für Familie, Senioren, Frauen und Jugend. *Alleinerziehende in Deutschland—Lebenssituationen und Lebenswirklichkeiten von Müttern und Kindern*. 28th ed.

Campbell, Claudia. "Das Verbot der Leihmutterschaft." *Neue Juristische Wochenschrift–Spezial* (2018): 196.

Dethloff, Nina. "Reform des Kindschaftsrechts." *Neue Juristische Wochenschrift* (1992): 2200.

Dethloff, Nina, and Rudolf Gerhardt. "Ein Reproduktionsmedizingesetz ist überfällig: Zuordnung des Kindes zu den Wunscheltern nicht zum Samenspender." *Zeitschrift für Rechtspolitik* (2013): 91.

Deutsches IVF Register. *Jahrbuch 2016*.

Donellus, Hugo. *Opera Omnia: cum Notis Oswaldi Hilligeri*. Florence, 1840–47.

Frank, Rainer. "Brauchen wir Adoption." *Zeitschrift für das gesamte Familienrecht* (2007): 1693.

Gelashvili, Irma. "Legal and Ethical Problems of Surrogacy." *Tbilisi State University Journal of Law* (2011): 77.

Grziwotz, Herbert. "Künstliche Fortpflanzung und Vertragsgestaltung (Kinderwunschverträge)." In *Künstliche Fortpflanzung und europäisches Familienrecht*, edited by Anatol Dutta et al., 25–58. Bielefeld: Gieseking, 2015.

Grziwotz, Herbert. "Recht auf Stiefkindadoption in faktischen Lebensgemeinschaften?" *Neue Juristische Wochenschrift* (2017): 1646.

Harder, Franz. "Wer sind Vater und Mutter?" *Juristische Schulung* (1986): 505.

Heiderhoff, Bettina. "Rechtliche Abstammung im Ausland geborener Leihmutterkinder." *Neue Juristische Wochenschrift* (2014): 2673.

Helms, Tobias. "Künstliche Fortpflanzung und Internationales Privatrecht." In *Künstliche Fortpflanzung und europäisches Familienrecht*, edited by Anatol Dutta et al., 59–80. Bielefeld: Gieseking, 2015.

Helms, Tobias. "Rechtliche, biologische und soziale Elternschaft—Herausforderungen durch neue Familienformen." *Neue Juristische Wochenschrift–Beilage* (2016): 49.

Helms, Tobias, and Andreas Botthof. "Die Volljährigenadoption als Mittel der Nachlassplanung—Plädoyer für die Einschränkung eines anachronistischen Rechtsinstituts." In *Zivilrecht und Steuerrecht, Erwerb von Todes wegen und Schenkung: Festschrift für Jens Peter Meincke zum 80. Geburtstag*, edited by Karlheinz Muscheler and Reinhard Zimmermann, 143–62. Munich: Beck, 2015.

Kindler, Heinz, Sabine Walper, Ulrike Lux, and Ina Bovenschen. "Kenntnis der Abstammung bei fragmentierter Elternschaft aus humanwissenschaftlicher Sicht." *Neue Zeitschrift für Familienrecht* (2017): 929.

Krause, Frank-Werner. "Die Volljährigenadoption: Probleme der Adoption Erwachsener und deren Lösung de lege lata und de lege ferenda." Diss., University of Freiburg, 1971.

Kunst, Christiane. *Römische Adoption: Zur Strategie einer Familienorganisation*. Frankfurt: Marthe Clauss, 2006.

Löhnig, Martin. "Die Leihmutterschaft in der aktuellen Rechtsprechung." *Neue Zeitschrift für Familienrecht* (2017): 546.

Löhnig, Martin. "Ehe für alle—Abstammung für alle?" *Neue Zeitschrift für Familienrecht* (2017): 643.

Löhnig, Martin. "Zivilrechtliche Aspekte der Samenspende de lege ferenda." *Zeitschrift für Rechtspolitik* (2015): 76.

Münchener Kommentar zum BGB. 7th ed. 2017/18.

(Muster-)Richtlinie zur Durchführung der Assistierten Reproduktion. 2006.

Mynsinger von Frundeck, Joachim. *Apoteslesma, sive corpus perfectum Scholiorum ad quatuor libros Institutionum Iuris civilis*. Basel, 1555.

Reinhardt, Jörg. *Adoptionsvermittlungsgesetz*. 4th online ed. 2017.

Richtlinie zur Entnahme und Übertragung von menschlichen Keimzellen im Rahmen der assistierten Reproduktion. 2017.

Roth, Andreas. "Der Ausschluss der Vaterschaftsanfechtung nach Einwilligung in die heterologe Insemination (§ 1600 Abs. 2 BGB)." *Deutsche Notar-Zeitschrift* (2003): 805.

Roth, Andreas. "Die Zustimmung eines Mannes zur heterologen Insemination seiner Ehefrau." *Zeitschrift für das gesamte Familienrecht* (1996): 769.

Schlieffen, Angela von. *Offene Adoptionen—Ein Grund zur Reform des Adoptionsrechts*. Berlin, 1996.

Schmidt, Christopher. "Anwendung von § 1592 Nr. 1 auf Co-Mütter?" *Neue Zeitschrift für Familienrecht* (2017): 832.

Schnitzerling, Manfred. "Die Fortentwicklung der Adoption seit der Jahrhundertwende." *Das Standesamt* (1960): 57.

Schott, Clausdieter. *Kindesannahme—Adoption—Wahlkindschaft: Rechtsgeschichte und Rechtsgeschichten*. Frankfurt: Wolfgang Metzner, 2009.

Schott, Clausdieter. "Sachsenspiegel und Adoption—die Macht der Glosse." *Zeitschrift für neuere Rechtsgeschichte* (2011): 1.

Sheehan, Michael. "The European Family and Canon Law." *Continuity and Change* (1991): 347.

Statistisches Bundesamt. *Statistiken der Kinder- und Jugendhilfe: Adoptionen*. 2015.

Tancred. *Summa de matrimonio*, edited by Agathon Wunderlich. Göttingen, 1841.

Taupitz, Jochen, and Julia Schlüter. "Heterologe künstliche Befruchtung: Die Absicherung des Samenspenders gegen unterhalts- und erbrechtliche Ansprüche des Kindes." *Archiv für civilistische Praxis* (2005): 591.

Wehrstedt, Stefan. "Notarielle Vereinbarungen anlässlich einer künstlichen Befruchtung." *Rheinische Notar-Zeitschrift* (2005): 109.

Wilms, Tobias. "Die künstliche Befruchtung in der notariellen Beratung." *Rheinische Notar-Zeitschrift* (2012): 141.

Zervogianni, Eleni. "Künstliche Fortpflanzung im griechischen Recht." In *Künstliche Fortpflanzung und europäisches Familienrecht*, edited by Anatol Dutta et al., 205–28. Bielefeld: Gieseking, 2015.

Zschiebsch, Mathias. "Welche Auswirkungen hat das Gesetz 'Ehe für alle' auf das Adoptionsrecht?" *notar* (2017): 363.

Acknowledgments

This little book has benefited enormously from two collaborative efforts I was engaged in in the recent past: my work on adoption with Martin Löhnig and my work on assisted reproduction with Christoph Moes. I owe both colleagues a debt of thanks. I would also like to thank my ever trusty *Lehrstuhl* team at Kiel University – especially Moritz Philipp Schulz, Svend-Bjarne Beil, Katharina Schnoor, Jasmin Baasch, Franziska Plath, and Laura Hannig – for their valuable assistance at the copy-editing stage.